The *Timeless Cork* route

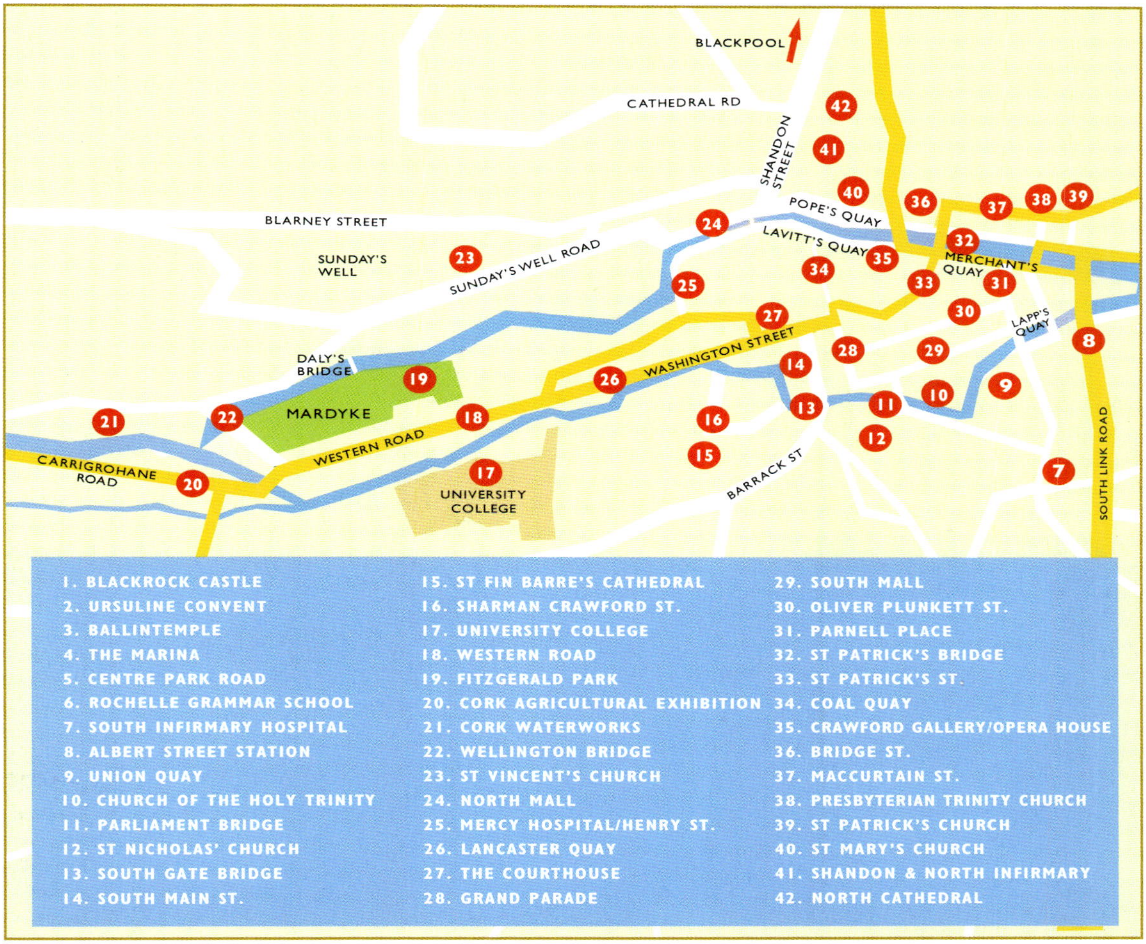

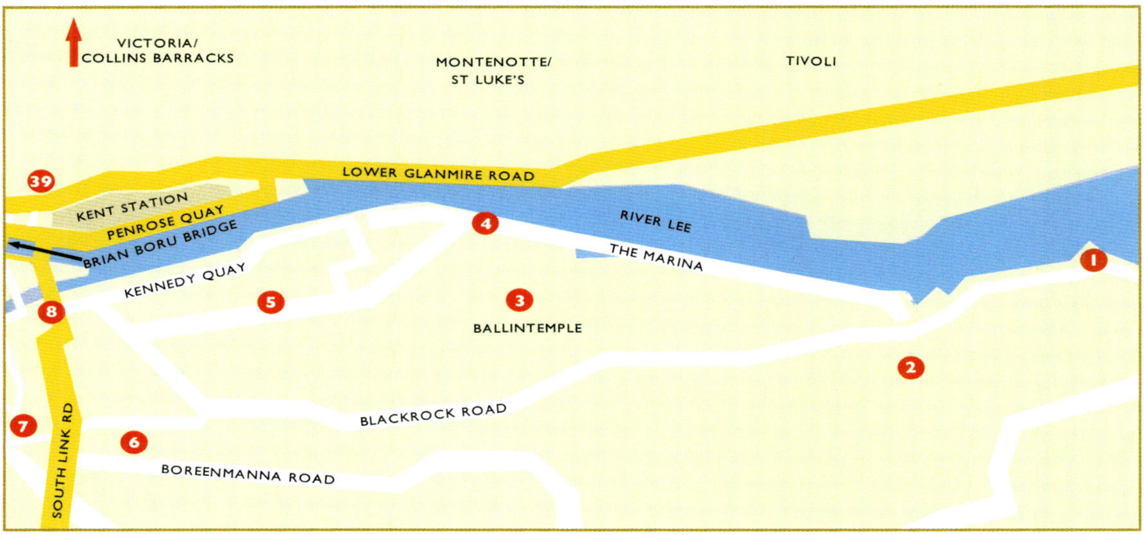

MERCIER PRESS
Cork
www.mercierpress.ie

ISBN: 978 1 78117 168 4

10 9 8 7 6 5 4 3 2 1

A CIP record for this title is available from the British Library

Printed and bound in the EU.

TIMELESS CORK

MICHAEL LENIHAN

MERCIER PRESS
IRISH PUBLISHER – IRISH STORY

To my wife Josephine,
son Andrew,
daughter Catherine,
grandson Culann
and granddaughter
Abigail.

Acknowledgements

This book would not have materialised without the assistance and kindness of the following people, so many thanks to Denis Lenihan for his wonderful contribution on the geographical locations of Cork city; Anita Lenihan and Tony Lenihan for their interest and helpful suggestions; Terry Atridge for her professional scanning of the old glass lantern slides; Niamh Twomey, Heritage Officer, Cork City Council; Ciara Brett, City Archaeologist; Dr Richard T. Cooke; Dr Donal O'Drisceoil of UCC; Antoin O'Callaghan; Tom Spalding; Pat Poland; The Cork Folklore Project; and the South Parish Historical Society. Their interest and encouragement made this book possible. I am deeply indebted to the following for kindly allowing me to use images from their collections: Charlie Ginnane, Lesley Roberts, Harry Ormond and Aine MacNamara, Archivist, Daughters of Charity. Tom Foley of the Blackpool Historical Society was extremely helpful providing images from the Society's records. And finally my thanks to Ronnie Herlihy, for his wonderful feedback and information on the city's history.

A special word of thanks to the staff of Mercier Press, whose unwavering support produced this magnificent book. To Sarah O'Flaherty, for her expertise in designing and formatting the book; Wendy Logue, who helped make sense of the captions; Patrick Dunphy, whose marketing skills are invaluable; Sharon O'Donovan, who is always helpful at the other end of the telephone; and Mary Feehan, for her continued support of my publishing endeavours.

And last, but not least, particular thanks to my wife Josephine, without whose help and understanding this project would never have seen the light of day.

Introduction

In 2011 I published *Pure Cork*, a book of images covering various aspects of the history of the city of Cork, of which I am a proud native. Overwhelmed by the positive reaction that the book received, I was encouraged to consider doing a follow-up, and the result is what you hold in your hand, *Timeless Cork*.

This time, rather than stick to simply splitting the images into categories, my publisher suggested that I might try to do a sort of illustrated tour of the history of Cork city, as if someone was taking a walk through the city's past. As it turns out, this presented more of a challenge than I had expected, and while I have tried to follow a logical route, the reader will see that in some places I have had to make a short detour to include all the interesting images that I have, and in others there is a little gap between destinations. I hope you will forgive me! The maps on the very first page of this book should help you follow my journey.

We start in Blackrock, before heading into the city and following a meandering route that covers many areas of both the north and south sides of the River Lee. The images date largely from the late nineteenth and early twentieth century, and many of them may be a surprise to the modern Corkonian. For instance it is hard to imagine what the reaction would be today if you came across a railway engine trundling through the centre of Cork as part of normal traffic, yet for a time this was a common sight on the streets of the city. And who can remember seeing a large group of pigs making an orderly crossing over St Patrick's Street? Moreover, many of the magnificent buildings which are shown in the book are no longer in existence, a rich architectural heritage lost forever. Other buildings, such as the Courthouse and the Quad in UCC, will be instantly recognisable, but I hope the captions provided with these images will prove of interest to the reader.

It is the nature of images from such a long time ago that they are limited in the subjects that survive to the present day. I have tried to provide as much of an overview of the city as I can and I hope the reader enjoys perusing this book as much as I enjoyed putting it together.

Michael Lenihan

A 'new and correct chart' of Cork Harbour drawn by the Rev. J. Lindsay of Her Majesty's ship *Fougueux*. The detail contained in the inset of this chart from 1759, 'A Continuation of Corke Harbour', shows us the starting point for our journey – Blackrock.

EAT ISLAND
East Passage
Belgrove
Temple Robin
Rahcorgey
Glanmore
Marloage Pt.
Golds Pt.
Fauras
To the Right Hon.ble
George Lord Anson.
Rt. Hon. Edwd. Boscawen.
George Hay LLD.
Thos. Orby Hunter Esqr.
Gilbt. Elliott Esqr.
Hon. Jno. Forbes Esqr.
Hans Stanley Esqr.
LORDS COMMISSIONERS
for Executing the Office of
Lord High Admiral of Gt. Britain.
This Chart is most humbly
Dedicated by their Lordships
most Obedient Servant
John Lindsay
Rostellan the Earl
of Inchiquins Seat
CLOYNE
Aghada
Rostellan Cove
A Scale of three English
MILES.
Little
Island
A Continuation of
CORKE HARBOUR
from a smaller Scale.
Carrickhowel Castle
Pt. of Great Island
English Miles.
Hawkes Rock
Note Be carefull to avoid having Roches Tower & Dogs Nose in one; for without the Tower, in that line, there is a small Rock, which will take you up at 23 feet water with 7 fathom round it.
The Figures, shew the depth in feet at low Water.
Balle Cotton
k the Old Head W b S 7 Miles. Cork Harbour mark'd

This wonderful postcard evokes the magic of Blackrock Castle. In former years the village of Blackrock was renowned for its fishing, but today it is better known for this famous landmark, which now houses its own observatory. The old castle on the site was destroyed by fire in 1827. The architects responsible for the rebuilding, James and G. R. Pain, added three additional storeys to the original tower and rebuilt the out-buildings. The rebuilding costs were £1,000. The castle was used from the Norman period as a lighthouse to guide shipping up the river.

The magnificent building of the Ursuline Convent, Blackrock. Built by Christopher Tuckey in 1720, who named it 'Pleasant Fields', and extended by Ruben Harvey, a Quaker merchant, in 1770, it was purchased by the Ursulines in 1824 from William Teulon, a Cork silversmith.

An interior view of the building from around 1900. The building was used by the Ursuline community to run a secondary school for girls.

Ballintemple, meaning the town of the church, has changed little since this photograph was taken. The tram followed a route that ran from Blackrock to the city centre. In the early 1800s Ballintemple Corporation was formed as a satirical alternative to lampoon Cork Corporation and their extravagant waste of taxpayers' money, in particular the lavish banquets hosted by the city mayors.

The Marina was, and remains, a very popular destination with Corkonians. The popular 1950s song 'Let's all go down The Marina' by Jerry Bruton is a reflection of this. Formed using material dredged from the river in about 1763, the area was originally known as the New Wall and Navigation Walk. In 1780 the corporation renamed it 'The Marina'. It is still home to the headquarters of the Shandon Boat and Lee Rowing Clubs. Unfortunately the lovely bandstand in the centre of this image has since disappeared from the landscape.

This photograph does justice to the grandeur of the beautiful tree-lined walk of The Marina. In the 1370s, thanks to Professor John Murphy of Queen's College Cork, hundreds of elm trees were planted along the walk, creating a wonderful ambience.

Edwardian ladies take their charges for a walk along The Marina, complete with a large perambulator. The shady walkway was the perfect place to stroll and get a little exercise.

The Irish Dunlop Co. Ltd factory on the Centre Park Road was founded in 1935 and was purpose built for Dunlop by the Cork building firm Sisk & Co. It was once one of Cork's foremost employers, just like its neighbour Ford. Prior to its closure in 1983, 850 men and women were employed there. This image of the factory comes from a commercial directory for 1953–56.

Dunlop manufactured all types of tyres for the Irish market.

This image shows part of the assembly line of the factory in the 1930s. The female employee is carefully preparing the steel beading necessary to bind the rubber compound to the tyres. To the right a group of visitors to the plant seem very interested in the process.

Ford's Works, Cork.

This postcard shows Henry Ford's wharf around 1920. Ford's factory, which was next to Dunlop's, covered a large area from the Centre Park Road down to the riverside. The crane on the left could be manoeuvred up and down the wharf as it was on a rail system. The ships that docked at Ford's wharf unloaded parts and loaded finished vehicles for export.

Henry Ford initially manufactured tractors at his Cork works, as there was a huge demand for these machines during the First World War. The mechanisation of farming had led to the replacement of horses with tractors, which could easily do the work of three to four horses in a day. This image shows Lord Mayor Tomás MacCurtain in March 1920 on a visit to the plant, just prior to his assassination by the RIC. (Courtesy of Fionnuala Mac Curtain)

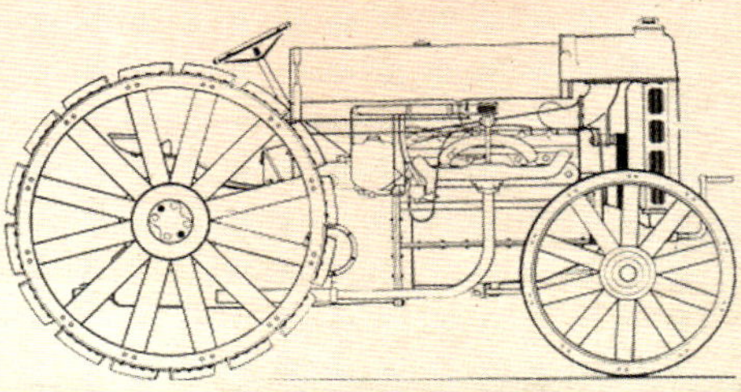

The final assembly line at the Ford factory, where the finishing touches are being made to a Ford Prefect as it rolls off the ramp. By 1933 production had switched from tractors to cars and commercial vehicles. This image was taken around the 1950s. The factory closed in July 1984.

HENRY FORD
CORK, IRELAND

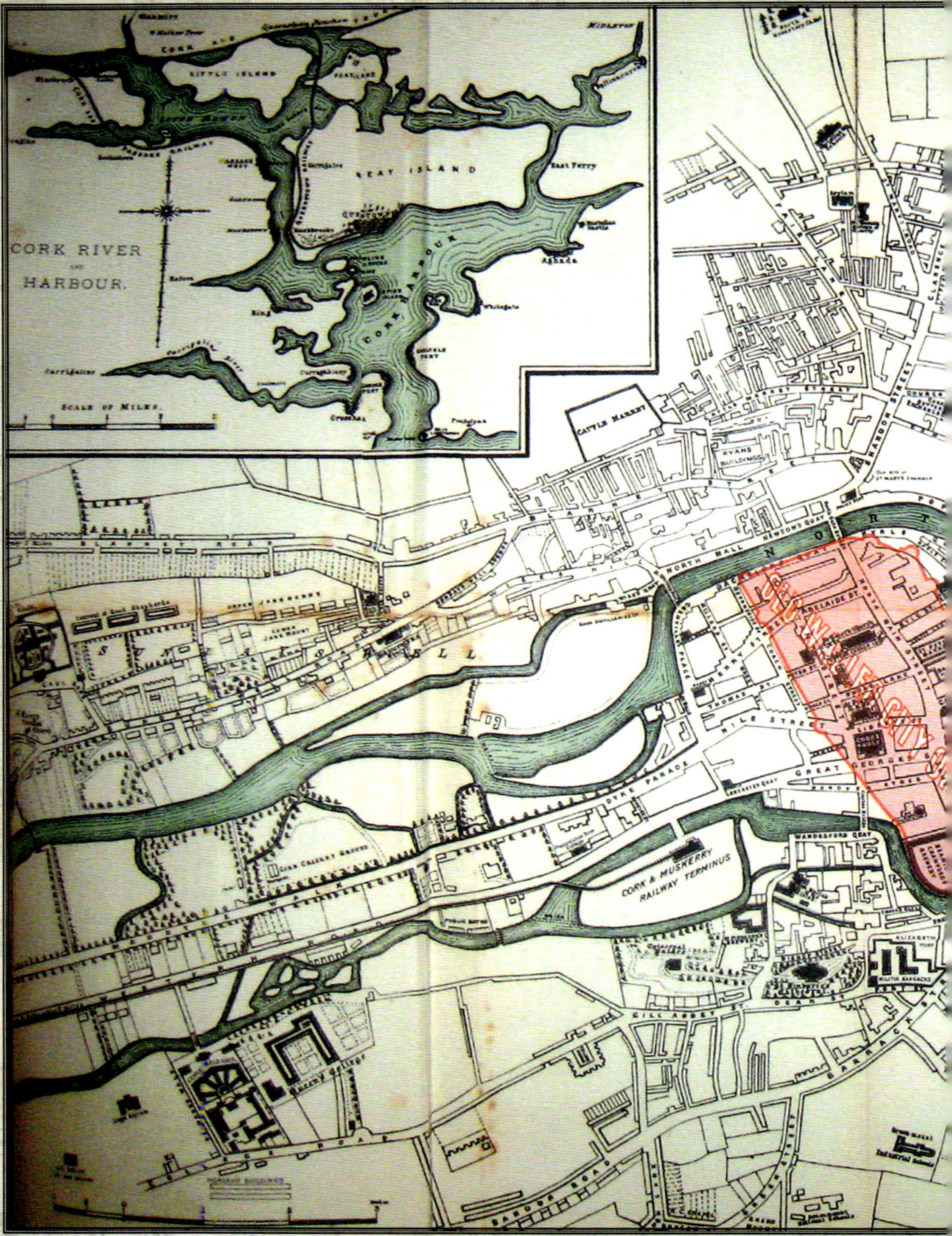

A map of Cork printed in 1893 by the Cork printers Guy & Company showing the old walled medieval city in red. This map was created just before the major changes that were about to take place towards the end of the nineteenth

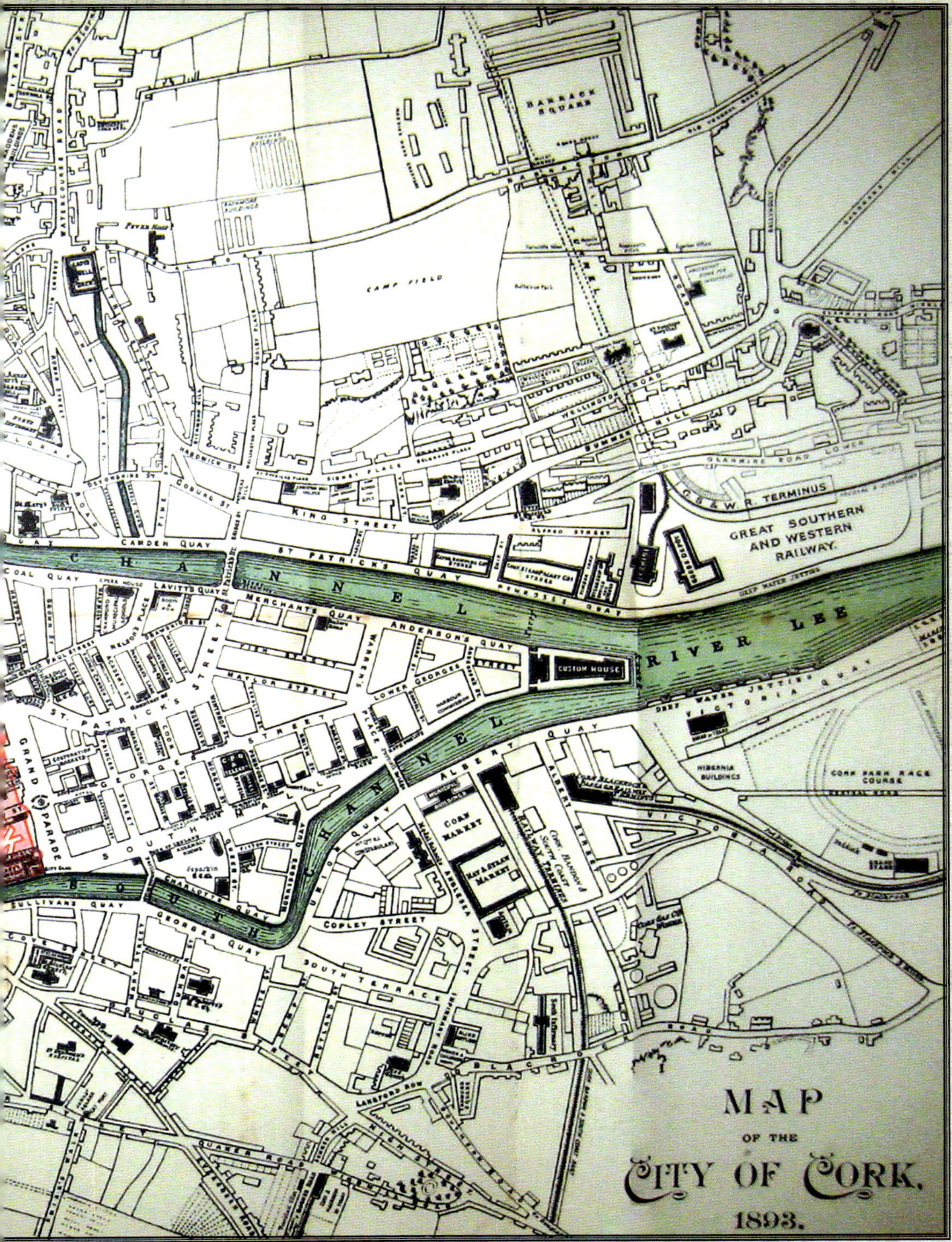

century with the arrival of mechanised transport. It also shows where some areas' names have changed, like Victoria Quay on the right which is now Kennedy Quay.

One of the Mayor of Cork's duties is to cast a large dart into the river symbolically claiming jurisdiction over the waters at the entrance to the harbour. This ceremony dates back to 1500, when King Henry VII granted the Mayor jurisdiction over the harbour, and is performed every three years. This image shows Lord Mayor Henry O'Shea carrying out this duty on 21 July 1914 and the tradition continues to the present day.

A wonderful picture of the Marina Mills owned by John Furlong & Company, flour millers, and constructed in 1891 on Victoria Quay. These were the first custom-built mills in the city and were designed by James McMullen, who came up with a more efficient method of milling flour by using steam-driven rollers in place of the old millstones. These formidable mills survived for nearly a century until they were demolished in 1986.

A nice view of Rochelle Grammar School, which was initially founded in 1841 as a seminary for young governesses and located on the Old Blackrock Road between the South Infirmary and Ashton School. Rochelle House was originally the home of Samuel Abbott, who owned the brewery at Fitton Street (now Sharman Crawford Street) from 1805. Unfortunately, this beautiful Georgian building was demolished during the excesses of the so-called 'Celtic Tiger' era.

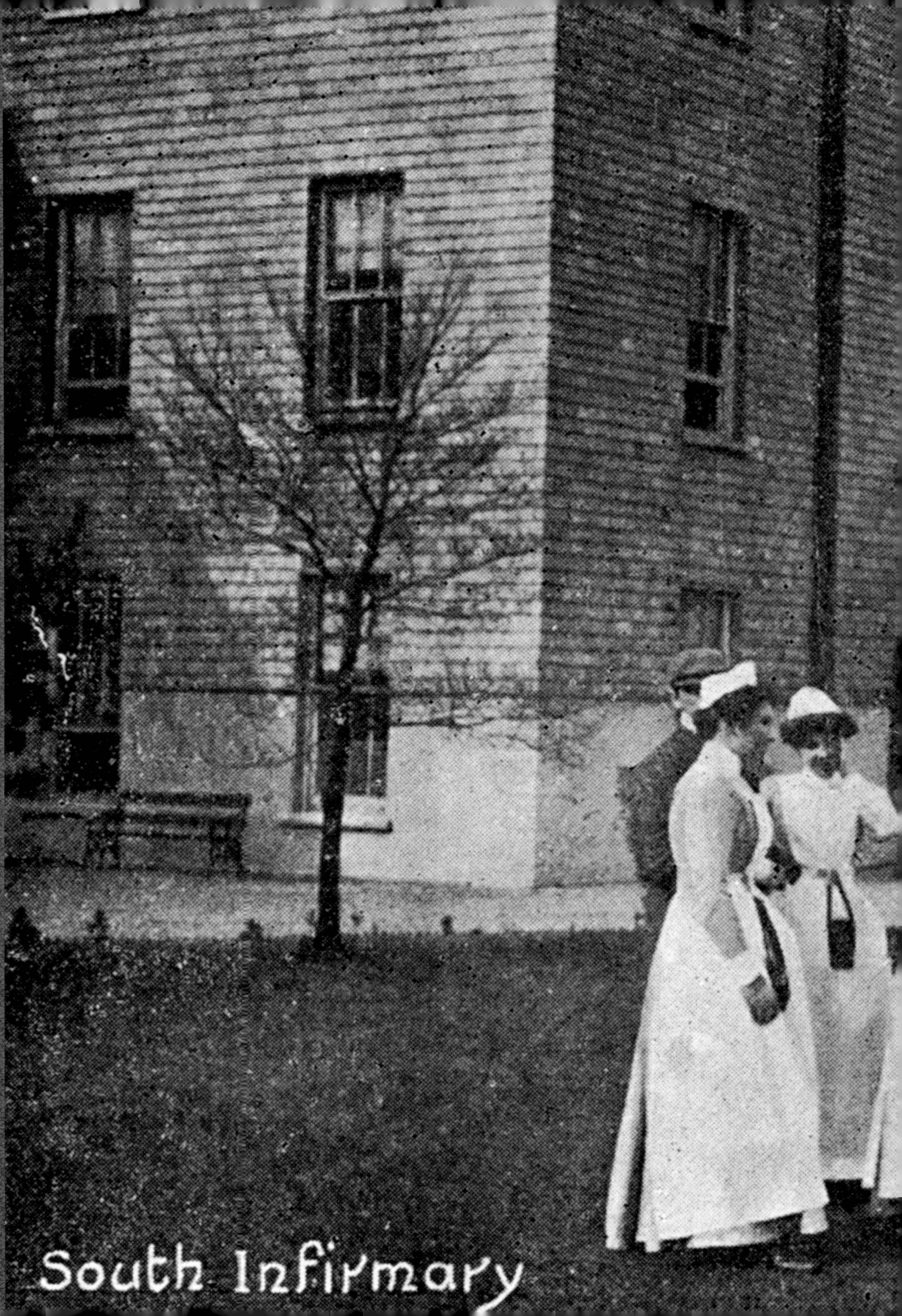
South Infirmary

A postcard of the South Charitable Infirmary, which was founded in 1761. In 1811 the first school of medicine in Cork was established in the infirmary by the surgeon John Woodroffe. This view shows the infirmary building with several medical staff, including nurses, *c.* 1910.

Left: Another view of the infirmary, taken by a local photographer, Brook Hughs, showing the extensive grounds that surrounded it in the early twentieth century. For many years charitable donations kept the hospital going and the list of subscribers included the cream of Cork society. The South Infirmary still exists today, but this original building is no longer there.

The Victoria Hospital, Cork

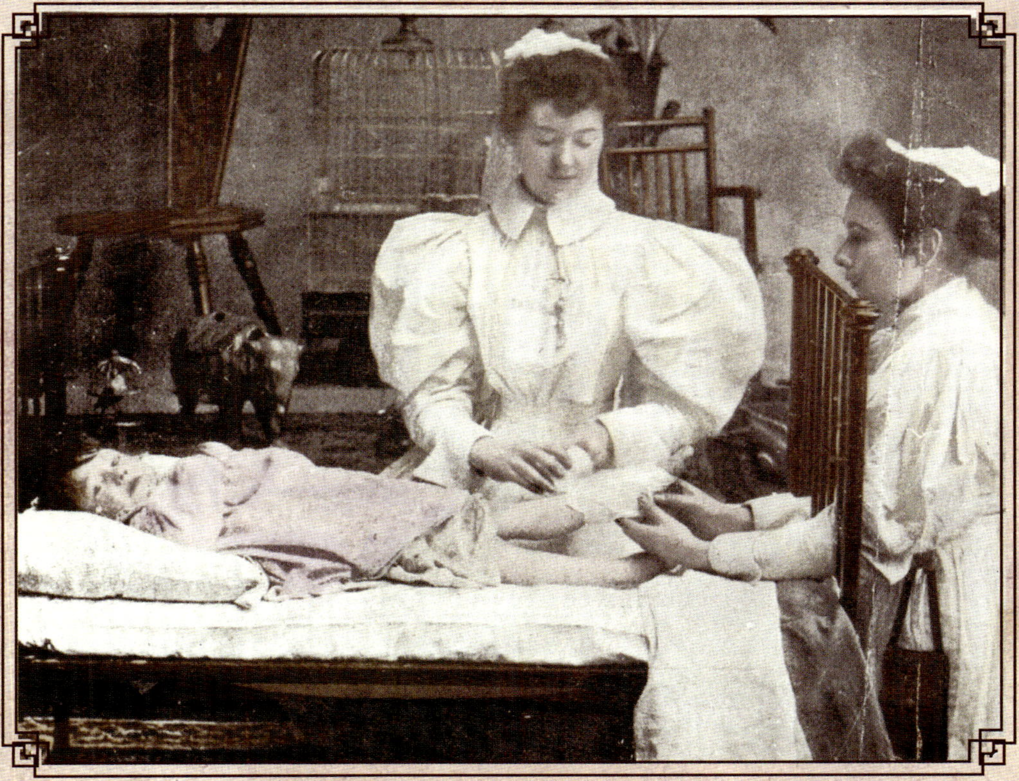

The Victoria Hospital, originally founded as 'The County and City of Cork Hospital' in 1874, was initially located at Union Quay. By 1885 it had relocated to Infirmary Road, next to the South Infirmary. In January 1988 the two hospitals amalgamated to become the present-day South Infirmary-Victoria University Hospital. The image above, dating to 1896, shows two nurses attending a young patient at Victoria Hospital. Up until 1914 male patients were not admitted to the hospital, but this changed during the First World War, when twenty-eight wounded soldiers and four officers were successfully treated there.

Funds Urgently Required for Hospital Improvements

Leo, the St Bernard, was the Victoria Hospital's mascot and was used for fund-raising. He became a firm friend of patients and patrons alike and featured on his own postcard, seen here. In 1896 he travelled as far afield as London to raise funds to clear a hospital debt of £700, incurred from an upgrade of the sanitation in the hospital. Considerable sums of money were collected through his fund-raising efforts.

This unusual photograph shows some young infants with their St Bernard friend. Note the child peering out from her hospital cot in the background.

A wonderful photograph of railway carriages on what is now the city end of the South Link Road, continuing the tradition of transport in this area. This image was taken near the old Gas Works in 1912 and it gives a great sense of the magnitude of the railways' operation in Cork.

The new Albert Street Railway Station. Designed by John Benson, this terminus was first opened on Thursday 6 February 1873 to replace the old terminus located at the northern end of Victoria Road. The Cork, Blackrock and Passage Railway operated a rail service from 1852 until its closure in 1932. This photograph shows an excited crowd anxious to board an excursion train leaving for the coast.

A wonderful coloured map by the Cork, Blackrock & Passage Railway Co. of the harbour, showing their routes by rail and by steamer from around the late 1880s. The rail route runs from Albert Street to Passage West, but was not the only service available. By this time the C.B.&P.R. Co. had purchased the Citizens River Steamer Company. They owned a fleet of four vessels: the *City of Cork*, *Citizen*, *Lee* and *Erin*. In 1904 the rail route was extended to Crosshaven, when it became possible to travel by railway steamship and return by train for an all-in fare.

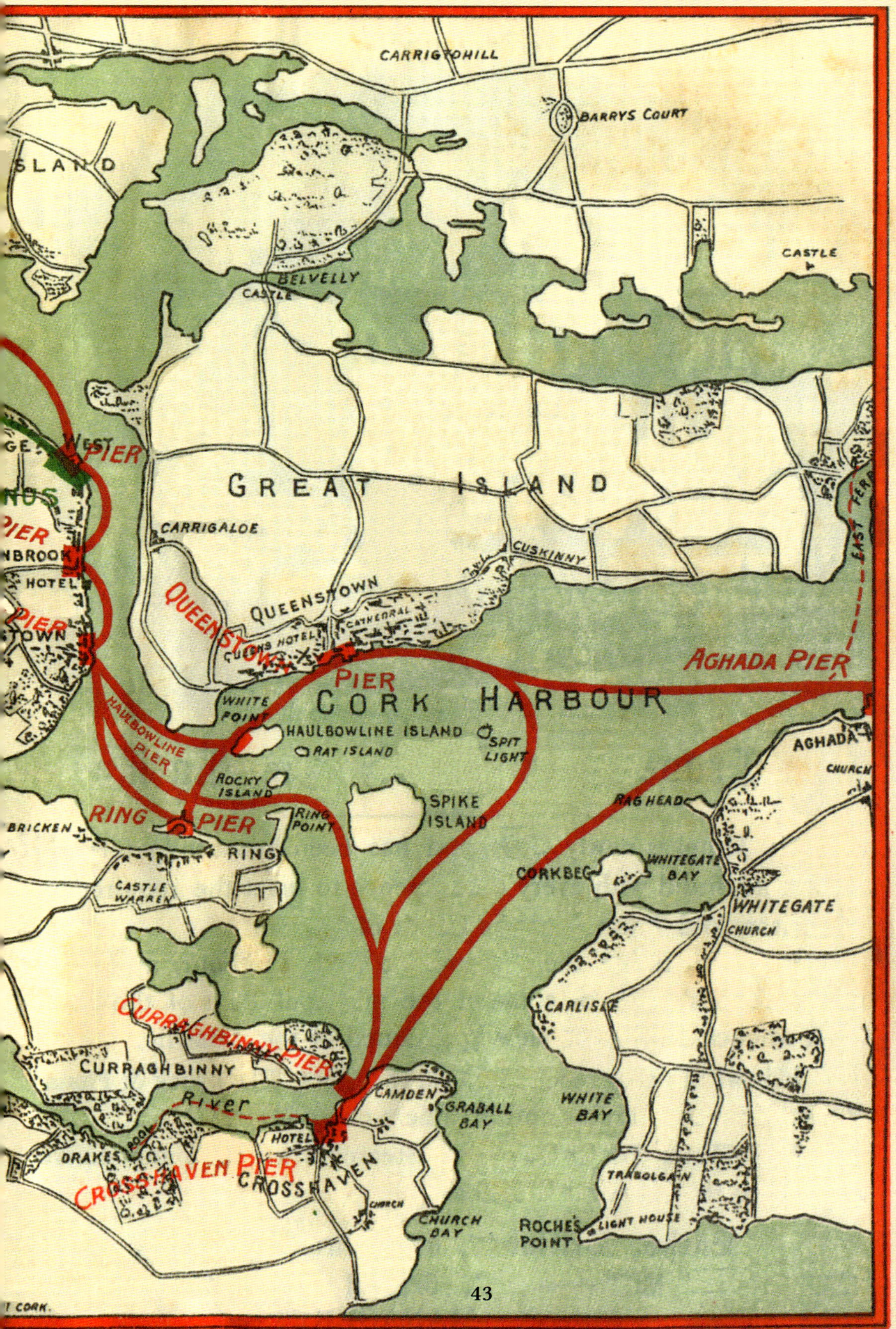

CARRIGTOHILL
BARRYS COURT
SLAND
CASTLE
BELVELLY
CASTLE
WEST PIER
GREAT ISLAND
CARRIGALOE
CUSKINNY
EAST FERRY
QUEENSTOWN
QUEENSTOWN
CATHEDRAL
QUEENS HOTEL
PIER
AGHADA PIER
WHITE POINT
CORK HARBOUR
HAULBOWLINE ISLAND
SPIT LIGHT
RAT ISLAND
HAULBOWLINE PIER
AGHADA
CHURCH
ROCKY ISLAND
RAG HEAD
SPIKE ISLAND
RING PIER
RING POINT
BRICKEN
RING
CORKBEG
WHITEGATE BAY
CASTLE WARREN
WHITEGATE
CHURCH
CARLISLE
CURRAGHBINNY PIER
CURRAGHBINNY
River
CAMDEN
GRABALL BAY
WHITE BAY
HOTEL
DRAKES POOL
CROSSHAVEN PIER
CROSSHAVEN
CHURCH
CHURCH BAY
TRABOLGAN
ROCHES POINT
LIGHT HOUSE

Union Quay, formerly known as Allen's Marsh, was renamed following the passing of the Act of Union between Britain and Ireland in 1801. The red-bricked RIC barracks on the right of this photograph was constructed in 1876. Following the Civil War it was set on fire by anti-Treaty forces and completely gutted, as can be seen in this image. It was rebuilt in 1926/1927, but did not survive to the present day.
(*Courtesy of Mercier Press*)

This panoramic view, taken from George's Quay *c.* 1900, shows Parliament Bridge, designed by William Hargrave and constructed in 1806, and the Capuchin Church of the Holy Trinity. The original church was designed by the architect George Richard Pain in 1832 and completed eighteen years later. The façade seen in this picture was not added until the start of the twentieth century. In the foreground we see a sailing ship moored at George's Quay of a type that was a common sight on the River Lee at this time.

IURCH & QUAY.

Design for Façade of Church of the Holy Trinity, Cork.

The Church of the Holy Trinity was built in 1850, but due to lack of funds and problems with the foundations there was no spire or portico. In 1891 a competition was held to design a façade for the church. This design by the noted Cork architect Arthur Hill was not chosen. It is interesting to see how the church might have looked, but also to note the striking similarities between Hill's plan and the actual building.

Lawrence, Publisher, Dublin.

Church of the Holy Trinity, CORK.

A view of the Holy Trinity from the well-known photographic studio of William Lawrence, Dublin, taken when the new façade was finished. Prior to the building of the ornate spire the church was a very modest structure with just a simple bell enclosure.

Moving further up the river, we look back at Parliament Bridge which links Sullivan's Quay to Parliament Street. The original bridge at this spot was badly damaged by a flood in 1804 and was replaced by this beautiful limestone structure in 1806. The Church of the Holy Trinity and the surrounding buildings provide the perfect backdrop for this coloured postcard.

Sullivan's Quay is situated in a very historic part of the city, as its western end is connected to Barrack Street, once the main southern approach to the city. The quay housed a fire station in the red-brick building with the white arch around the door, which closed in 1975 after the new Anglesea Street Station was opened. Another landmark of the quay was Sullivan's Quay National School, which was founded in 1928 and closed in 2006.

An unusual map which was used to promote St Nicholas' Church on Cove Street, above Sullivan's Quay. The location of the church and hours of service are shown. A church had existed on this site since medieval times and survived for many centuries until the siege of Cork in 1690. The present St Nicholas' was built in the Gothic Revival style and was designed by the architect Welland, with the steeple by Atkins. It was deconsecrated in the early 1990s and is now the home of the probation service. (*Courtesy of Lesley Roberts*)

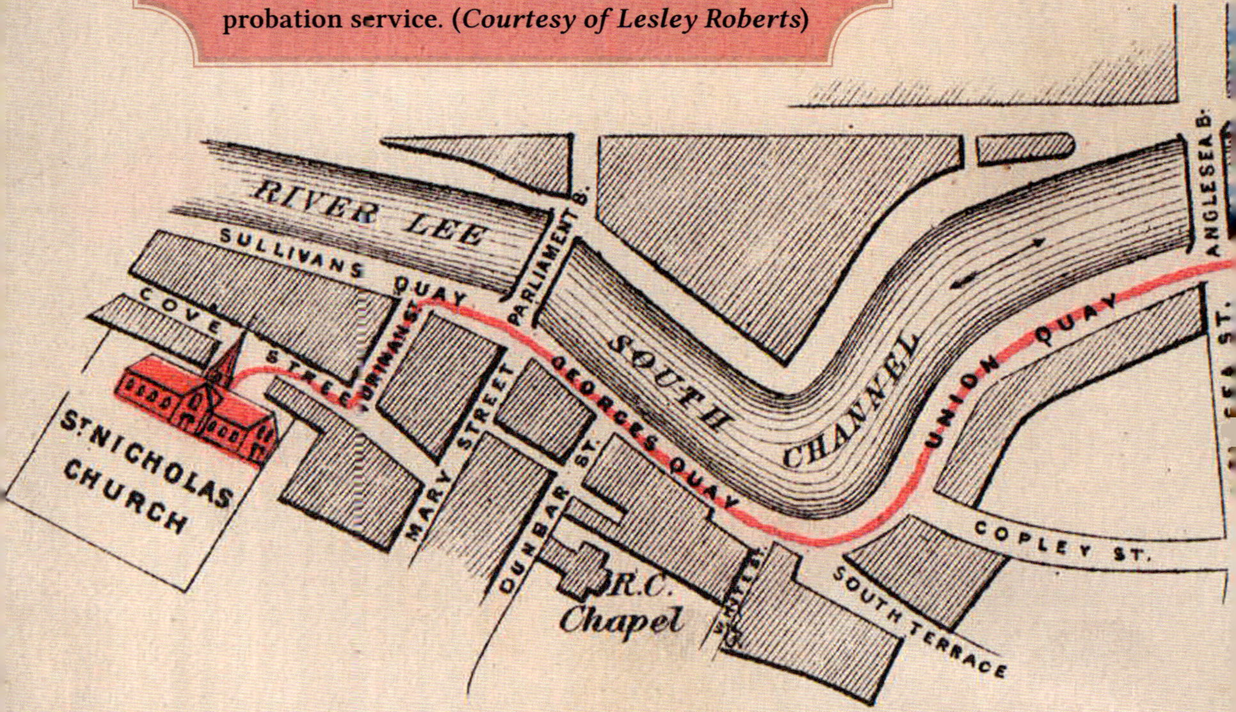

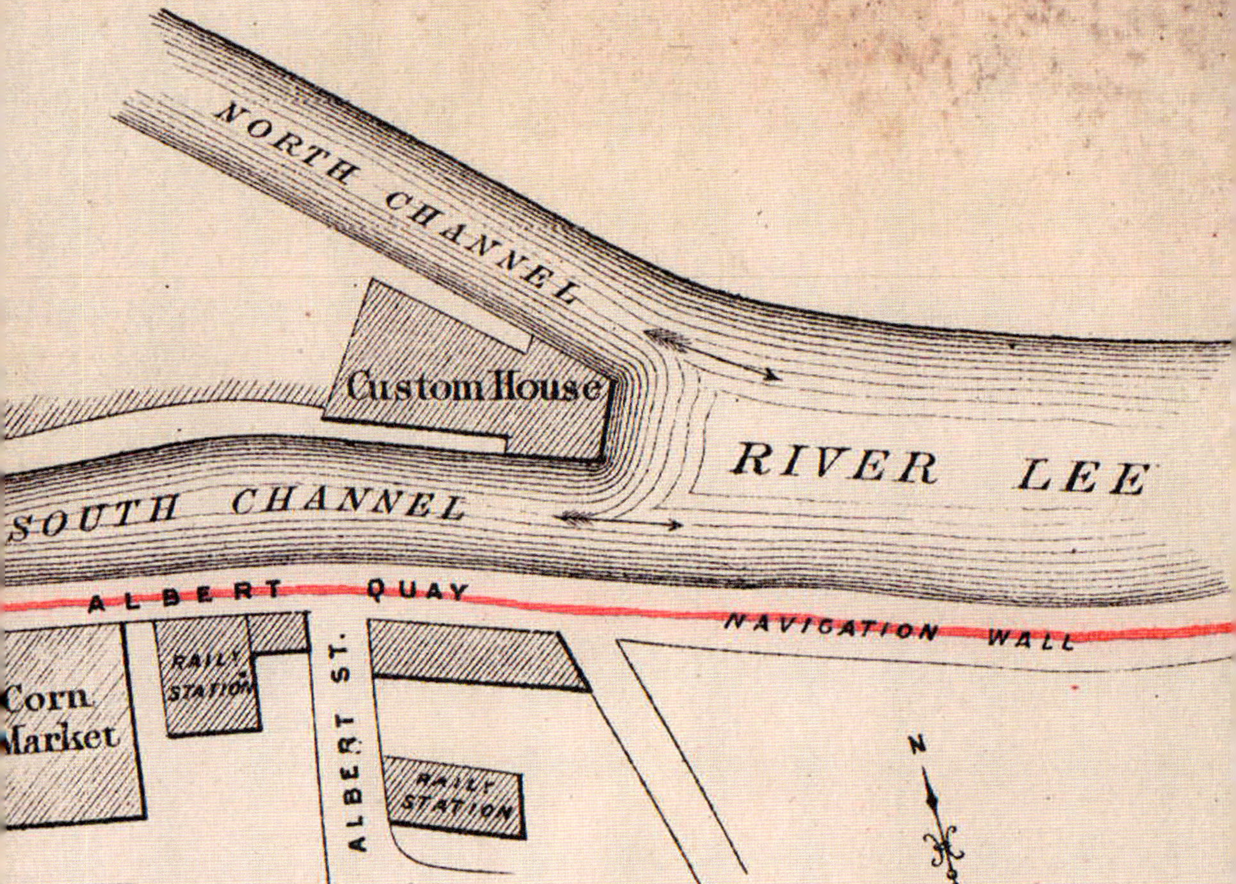

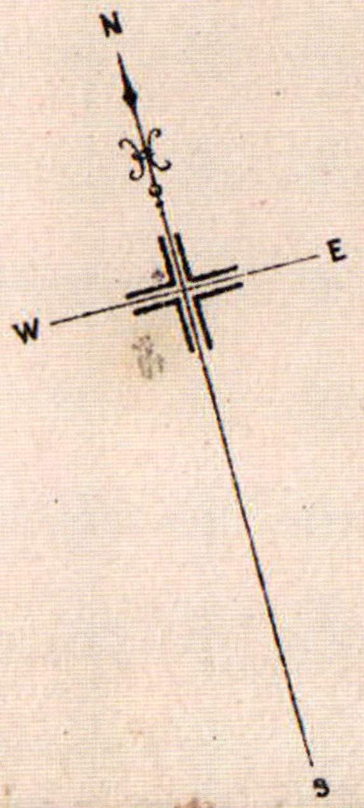

S. NICOLAS' CHURCH,

COVE STREET.

HOURS OF SERVICE.

Sunday Morning .... ¼ to 12 o'clock.
Sunday Evening .... 7 o'clock.
Wednesday Evening ...... 8 o'clock.

Route to the Church marked

The South Gate Bridge, which crosses from Sullivan's Quay to South Main Street, is Cork's oldest bridge. It was constructed in 1713. Beyond it, in this postcard from *c.* 1905, can be seen St Fin Barre's Cathedral, the jewel in Cork's architectural crown.

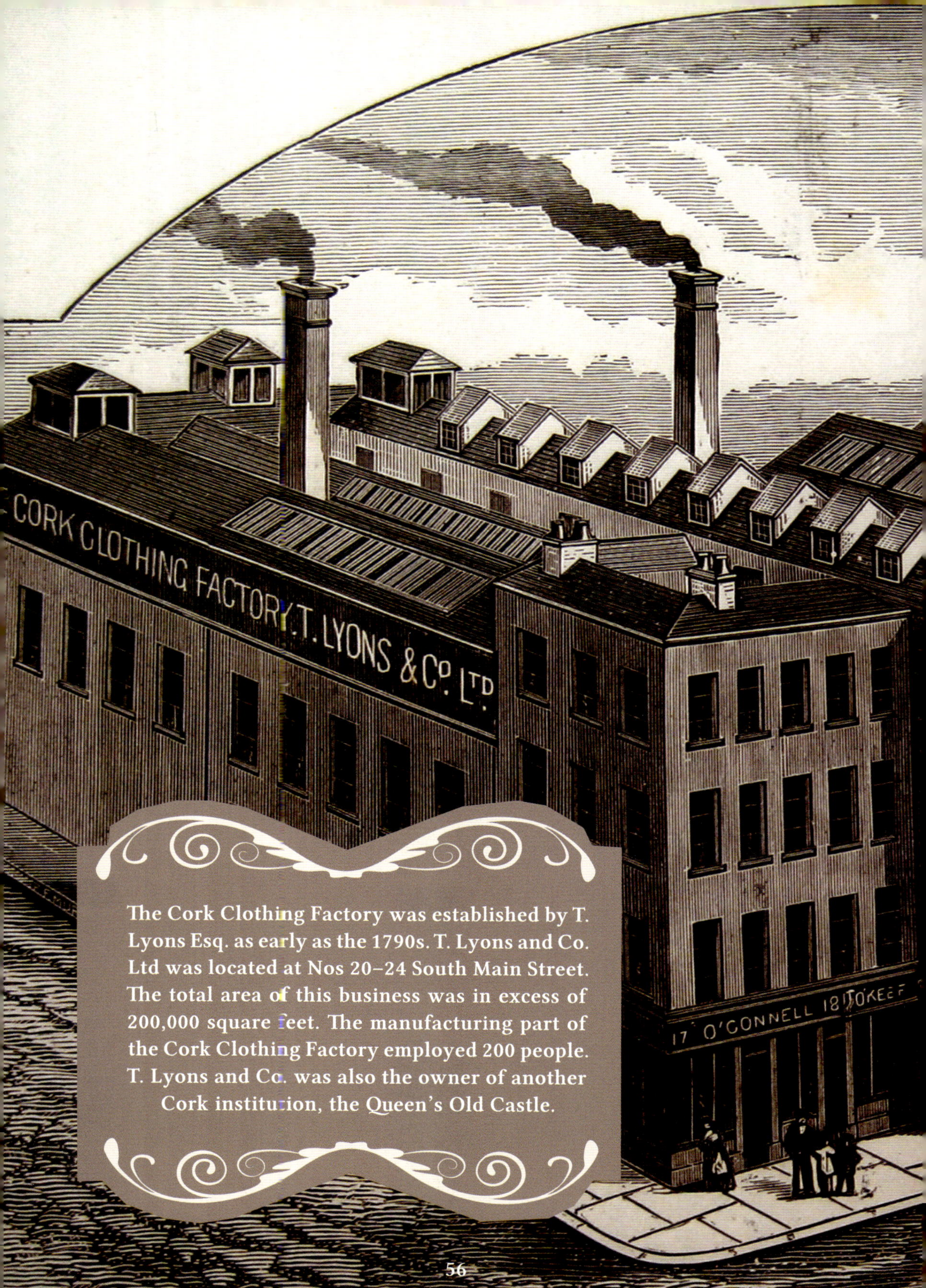

The Cork Clothing Factory was established by T. Lyons Esq. as early as the 1790s. T. Lyons and Co. Ltd was located at Nos 20–24 South Main Street. The total area of this business was in excess of 200,000 square feet. The manufacturing part of the Cork Clothing Factory employed 200 people. T. Lyons and Co. was also the owner of another Cork institution, the Queen's Old Castle.

20
21
22
23
T. LYONS & Co. LTD
WHOLESALE
WAREHOUSEMEN
& MANUFACTURERS
BROWN

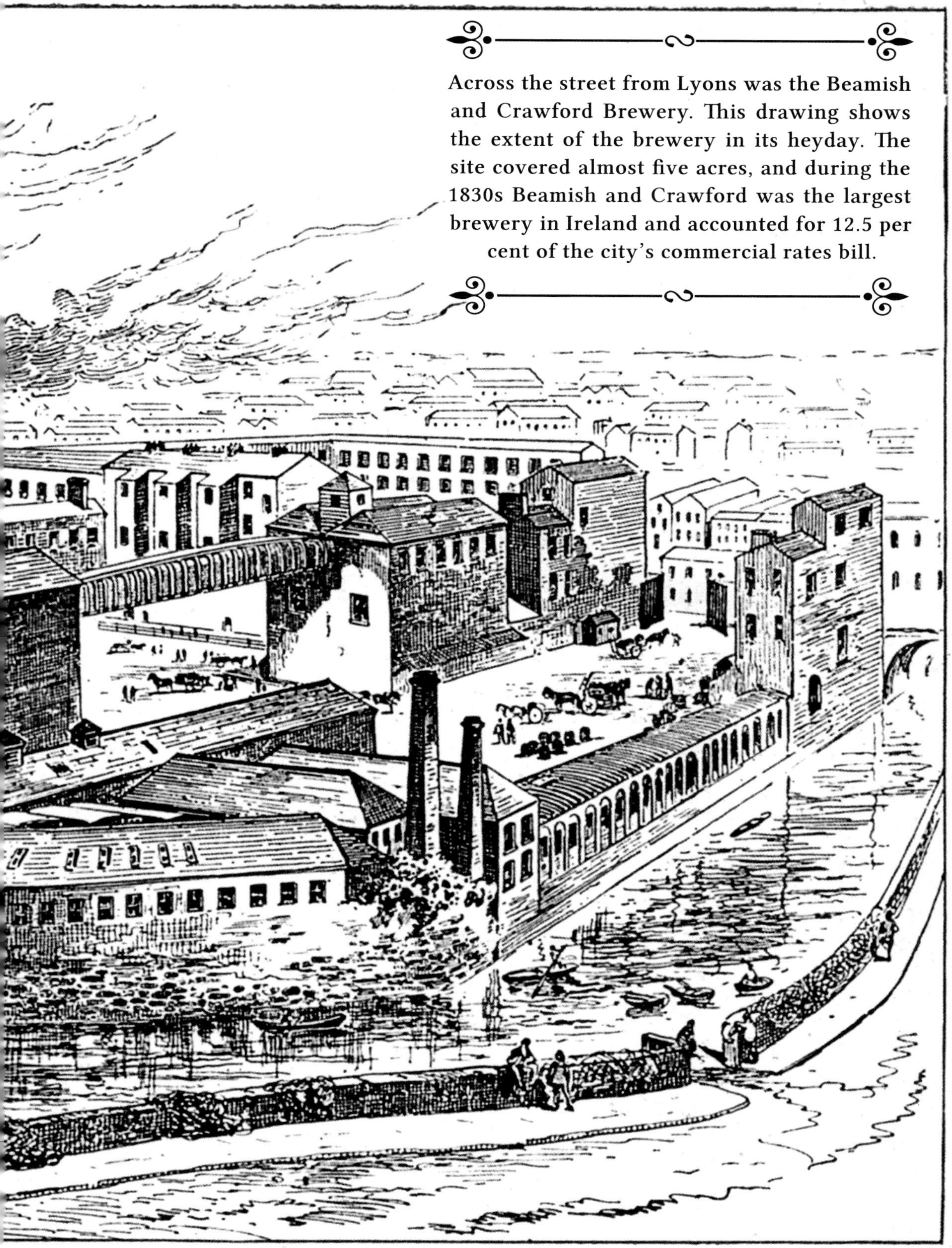

Across the street from Lyons was the Beamish and Crawford Brewery. This drawing shows the extent of the brewery in its heyday. The site covered almost five acres, and during the 1830s Beamish and Crawford was the largest brewery in Ireland and accounted for 12.5 per cent of the city's commercial rates bill.

This photograph shows the old coopering room of the Beamish and Crawford Brewery. The coopers in this photograph are working by natural light which was ideal for their intricate work. It is hard to believe that wooden barrels held together with iron hoops could contain gallons of stout and porter without leaking. The brewery is now sadly closed, although the site remains.

Heading back to the quays, we turn towards Proby's Bridge, St Fin Barre's Cathedral and Elizabeth Fort. This unusual view of the area was published in 1910 by the Stereo Travel Co., New York. To the right of the bridge a large area was set aside for the purpose of erecting billboard signage.

St. Fin Barre's Cathedral.

St Fin Barre's Cathedral has dominated the city's skyline since it was completed in 1877. The inset shows the old cathedral which was a simpler, smaller structure. The designer of the new cathedral building, William Burges, proudly proclaimed that the west front of the building would provide a specimen of the best architectural sculpture the age could produce. He succeeded admirably with the magnificent sculptured figures of the wise and foolish virgins, the resurrection of the dead and the four beasts of the evangelists.

DESIGN FOR CORK CATHEDRAL,
SUBMITTED BY EDWD W. GODWIN, ARCHT

An elaborate design for the proposed cathedral submitted by English architect Edward William Godwin. This was similar in many ways to Burges' winning design. The rules of the competition dictated that the expenditure was not to exceed £15,000, but the ambitious Burges exceeded that budget by over £85,000.

An image from *c.* 1900 of the new cathedral. The cathedral was built to replace the existing structure which had become unsuitable for worship. A sum of £8,500 was collected at the outset and fund-raising drives continued for many years as the building budget soared out of control.

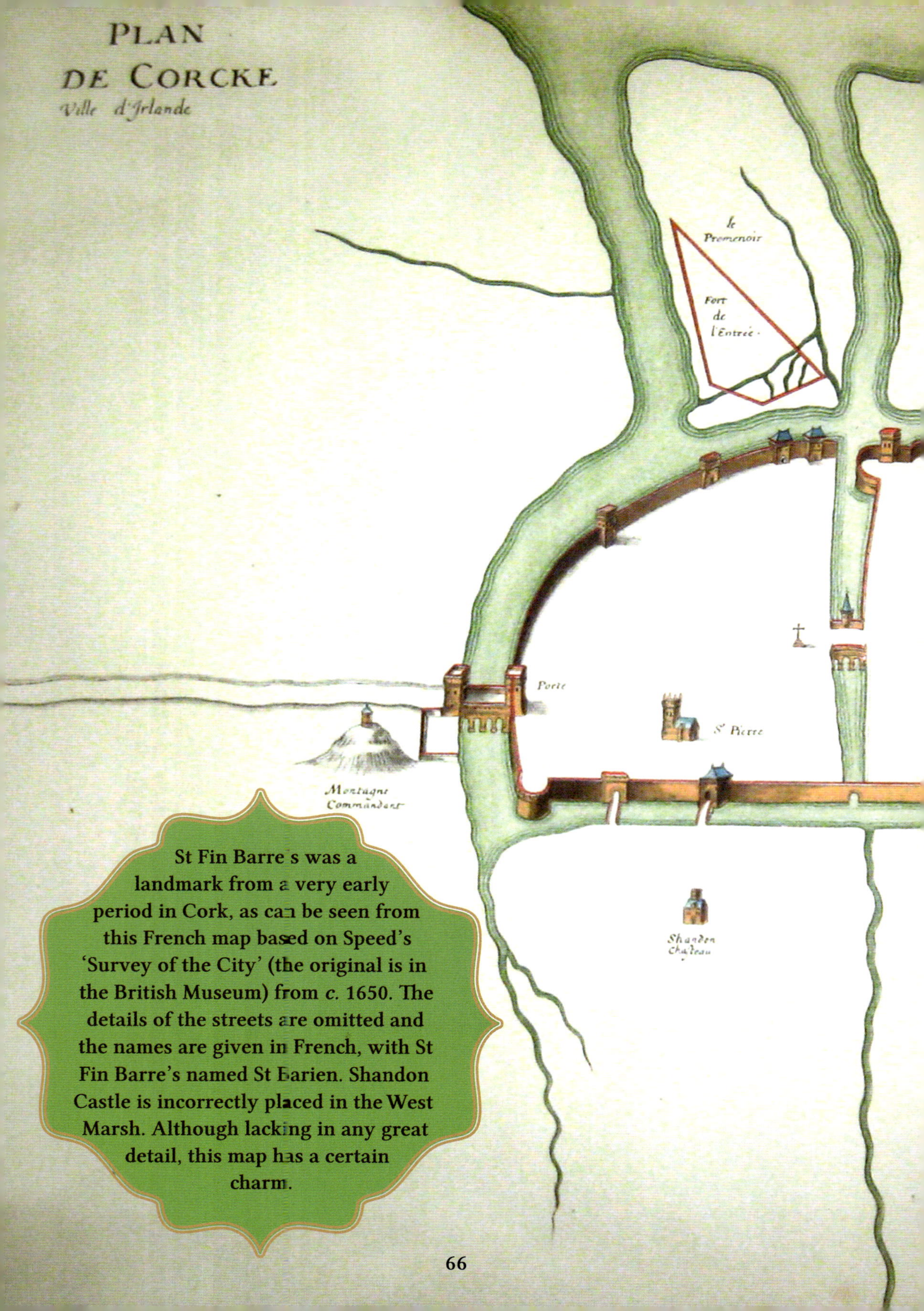

St Fin Barre's was a landmark from a very early period in Cork, as can be seen from this French map based on Speed's 'Survey of the City' (the original is in the British Museum) from *c.* 1650. The details of the streets are omitted and the names are given in French, with St Fin Barre's named St Barien. Shandon Castle is incorrectly placed in the West Marsh. Although lacking in any great detail, this map has a certain charm.

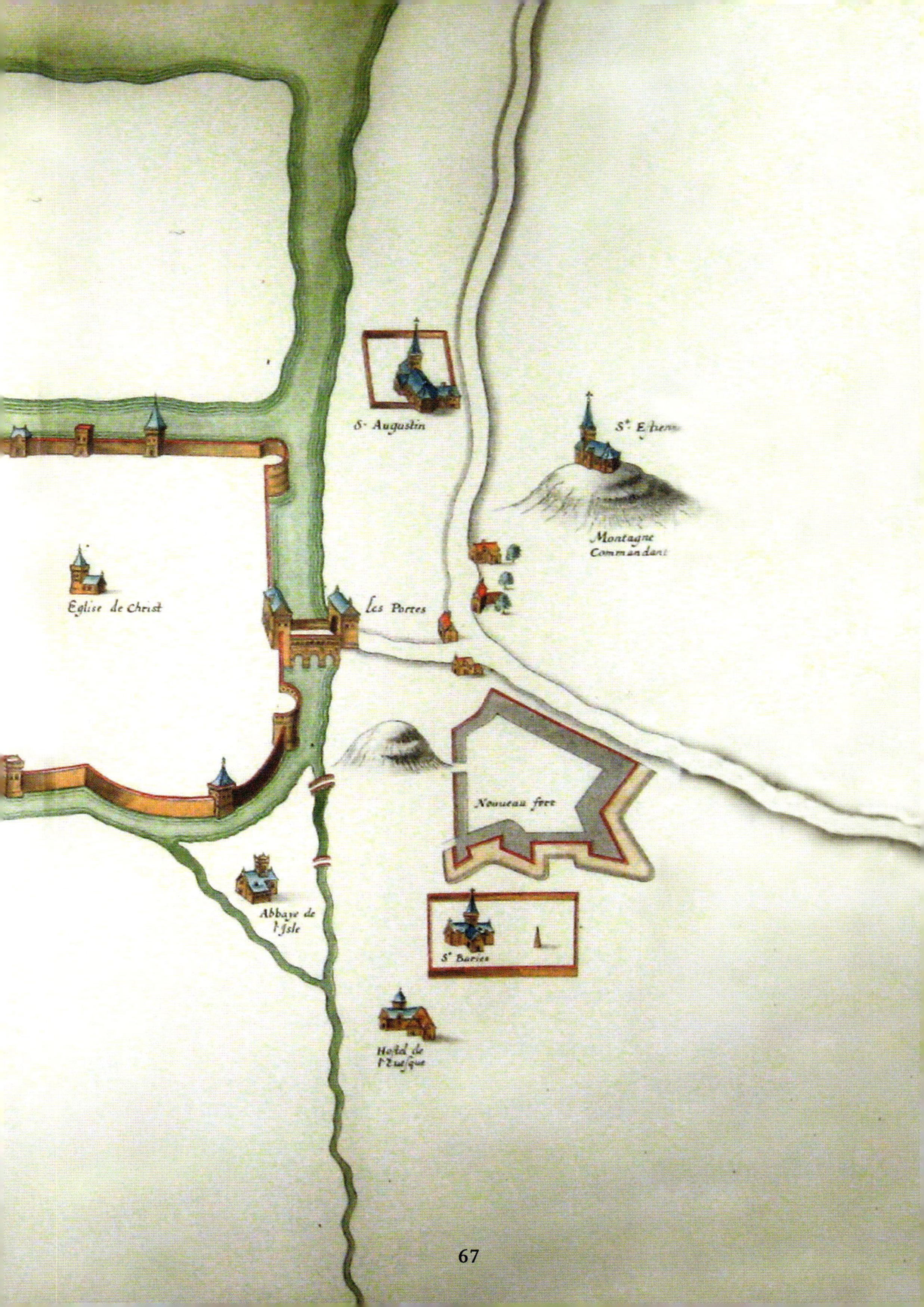
S. Augustin
St. Etienn
Montagne
Commandant
Eglise de Christ
Les Portes
Nouueau fort
Abbaye de
l'Isle
St Baries
Hostel de
l'Euesque

An image of the old Arnott's Brewery, now the site of the CIT Crawford College of Art and Design on Sharman Crawford Street. Murphy's Brewery purchased Arnott's in 1901 and promptly closed it to secure their grip on the local stout trade.

By 1906 no trace of Arnott's Brewery existed on the site at Sharman Crawford Street, as all the brewery buildings were totally demolished to make way for the Crawford Municipal Technical Institute. The building was designed by the Cork architect Samuel Hill and the site was donated by Arthur Frederick Crawford. The institute was formally opened by the Right Honourable Lord Mayor of Cork, Alderman James Simcox, on 16 January 1912 and in 2012 celebrated its centenary.

The beautiful stone-faced quadrangle of University College Cork, affectionately known as the Quad, was built between 1847 and 1849. The north wing of the Quad houses twenty-eight ogham stones dating from the fifth to the seventh centuries AD. This is the largest collection of its kind on public display in Ireland.

In the early morning of 15 May 1862, smoke and flames were seen coming from the roof and windows of the west wing of the college. By the time the fire brigade arrived the fire was out of control, although everything possible was done to contain it. The medical, engineering and agricultural departments were badly damaged. The mysterious fire became part of local folklore and the mystery of who started it remains.

A stereo view from the 1870s of the college, showing the beautiful limestone Quad building which was designed by the talented architects Thomas Deane and Benjamin Woodward. The building of the college had begun in 1845 and was completed in just four years, with a lavish opening ceremony held on 7 November 1849.

The old ferro-concrete bridge outside the entrance to University College was destroyed by flooding in 1916. The old bridge had stood on this site since 1879, when the Western Road entrance was built.

The plan of the front elevation of the Quad building.

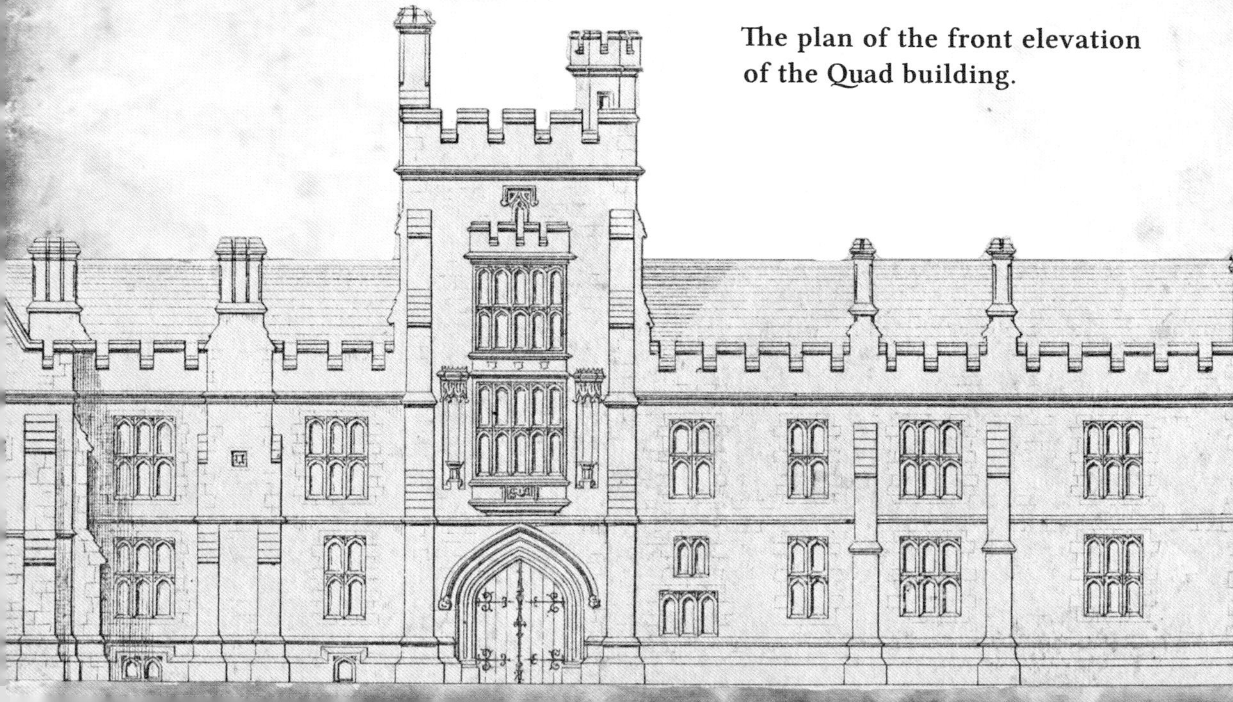

This aerial view of University College Cork shows the extent of the university grounds in the 1960s. The college was built on the site of the old county gaol. All of the old gaol buildings, some of which can still be seen here on the left, were eventually demolished to make way for the new college buildings.

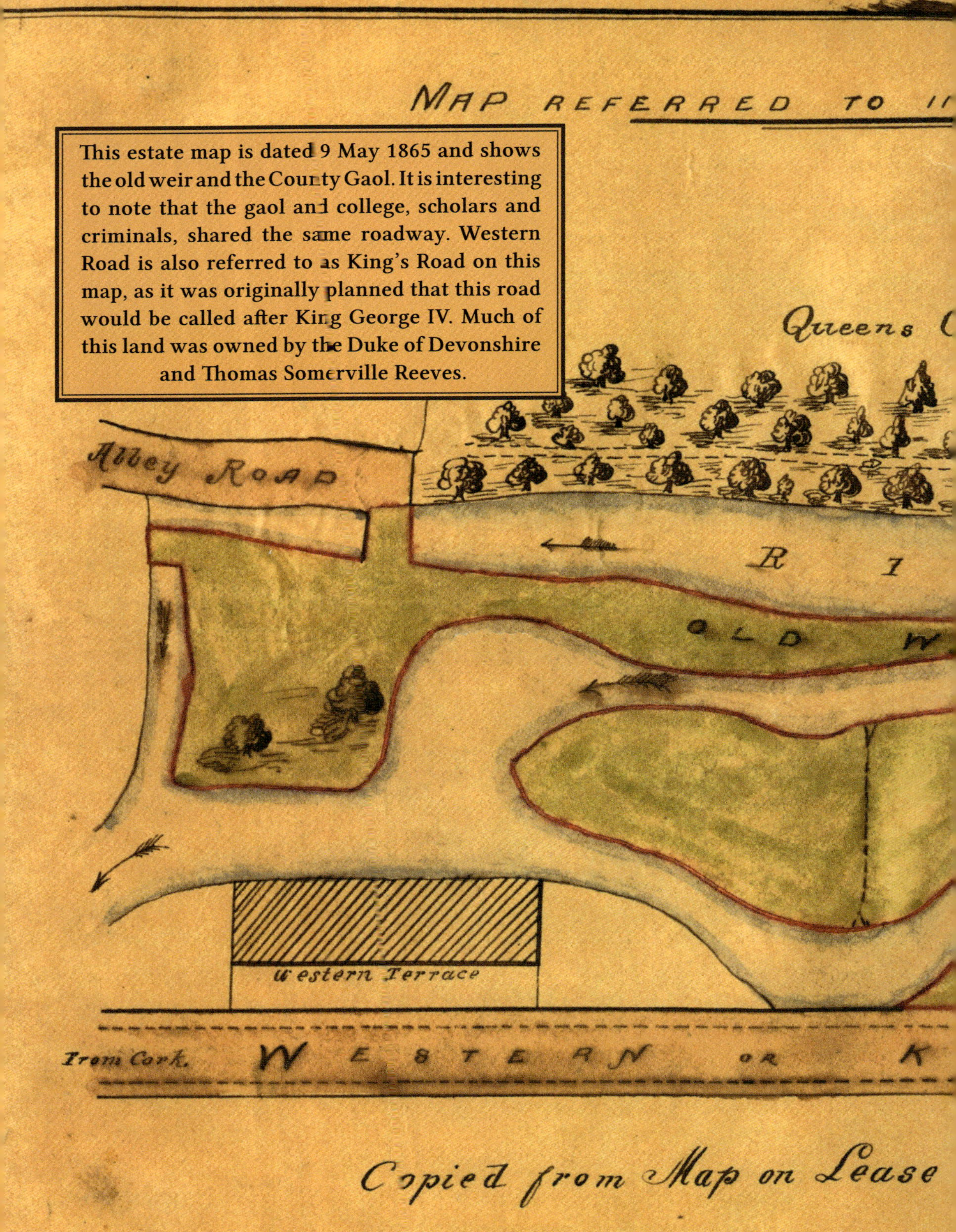

This estate map is dated 9 May 1865 and shows the old weir and the County Gaol. It is interesting to note that the gaol and college, scholars and criminals, shared the same roadway. Western Road is also referred to as King's Road on this map, as it was originally planned that this road would be called after King George IV. Much of this land was owned by the Duke of Devonshire and Thomas Somerville Reeves.

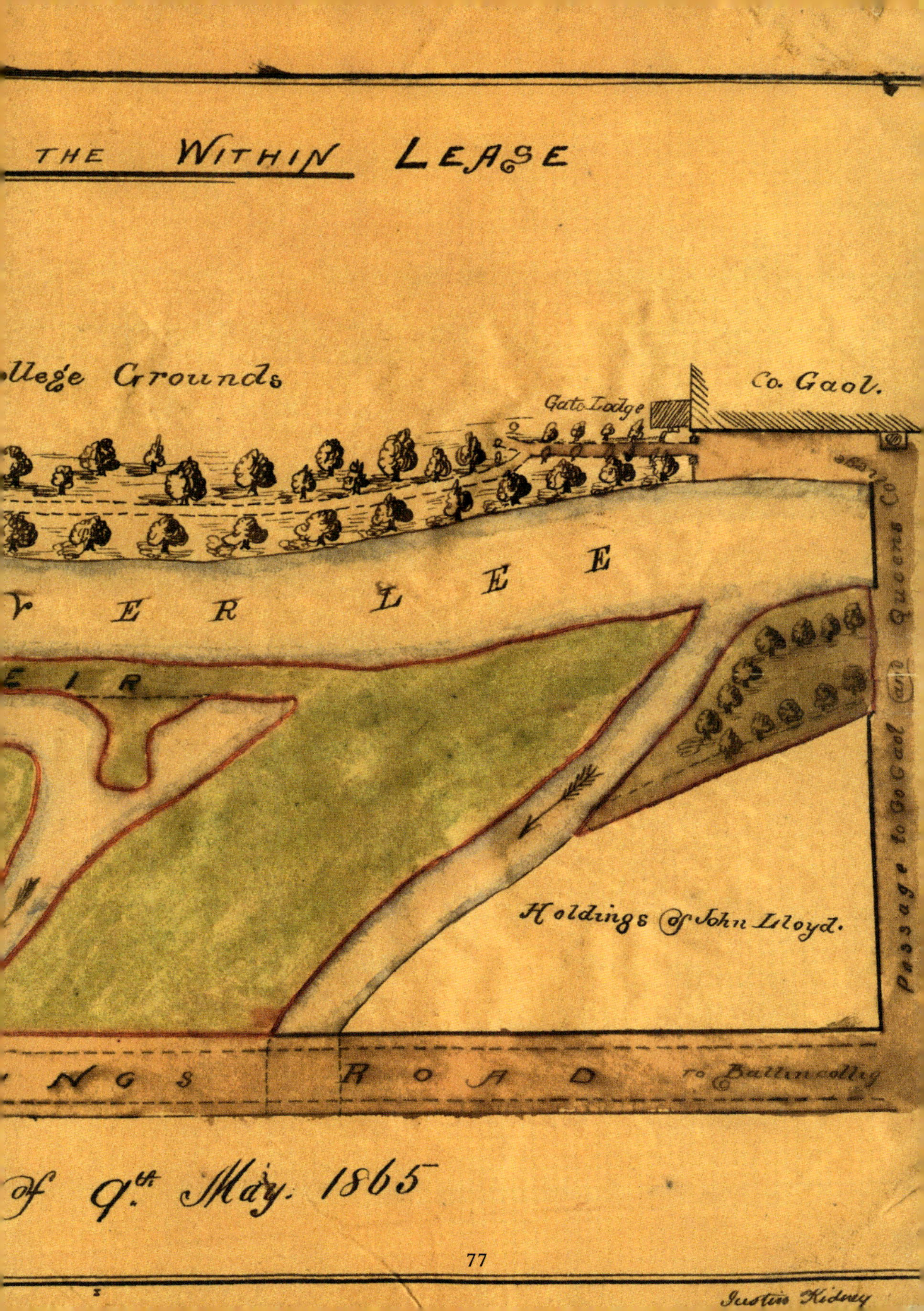

THE WITHIN LEASE
llege Grounds
Co. Gaol.
Gate Lodge
V E R L E E
E I R
Holdings of John Lloyd.
Passage to Co Gaol and Queens Co
N G S ROAD
to Ballincollig
of 9th May. 1865
Justin Kidney

CORK AND MUSKERRY LIGHT RAILWAY.

324.

Locomotive No. 7, which was called *Peake*, outside the old entrance to University College, which no longer exists. The locomotives on this line had their own identities, namely *The Donoughmore*, *The Muskerry*, *The City of Cork*, *St Anne's*, *Peake* and *Blarney*.

The three different modes of transport from the turn of the twentieth century are shown travelling along the Western Road in this postcard – a horse-drawn carriage, electric tram and steam locomotive. At times when the train and tram were aligned it looked almost as if a race was taking place between them. It

was originally planned that the Cork and Muskerry Light Railway would share Cork Electric's tram tracks and special chamfered wheels would be engineered to enable this. But long-running disputes between the companies ensured that locomotives and trams ran side by side instead.

Cricket Field the Mardyke, Cork.

An Edwardian postcard showing the cricket ground on the Mardyke, with St Vincent's, Sunday's Well, in the background. The cricket club was founded in 1849 on a site of five acres and is now the third oldest club in the country. The elegant finery worn by the ladies and gentlemen proclaim that this was indeed a fashionable place to be seen.

Fitzgerald Park was, and continues to be, a very popular destination for young and old alike. Following the success of the Cork International Exhibitions of 1902 and 1903 the area was turned into a public park. It was named in honour of Sir Edward Fitzgerald, the Lord Mayor of Cork who was the driving force behind the exhibitions.

The Mayor's Pavilion, shown here, is the only surviving building in the park from the 1902/1903 exhibitions. It is a quite an elaborate Art & Craft-style piece of architecture, as it was the first building near the entrance and was designed to impress the entering crowds. It is believed to have been designed by the architect Arthur Hill.

The Father Mathew fountain in Fitzgerald Park was constructed for the 1902 Cork International Exhibition and was originally located near the entrance of the exhibition grounds, now the main entrance to the park. After the event the fountain was relocated to its present position. This photograph dates to the 1950s, when Fitzgerald Park had become a very popular destination with Corkonians. The amusements, swings, slides and climbing areas, which still exist today, have provided great enjoyment for thousands of Cork children over the decades.

The Mardyke Walk was created by Edward Webber to lead people to his Red Tea House, which was built in 1722 in what are now the grounds of the Sacred Heart College. The child in this photograph from the 1930s sits astride a tricycle, a popular child's toy up until the 1960s, the majority of which were made by the Tri-ang company in Britain.

The beautiful Mardyke in the halcyon days in the early twentieth century, harking back to the time it was created by Edward Webber in 1726. Unfortunately the ornamental gates and the arches that spanned the avenue were removed by Cork Corporation in the 1950s, and most of the elms that lined the walk had to be cut down in the early 1970s due to an outbreak of Dutch Elm disease.

SUNDAYS WEL

An idyllic river scene of the Sunday's Well Boating and Tennis Club, which was founded in 1889. Despite its name, it is located off the Mardyke Walk, near the entrance to Fitzgerald Park. Regattas were traditionally held on the River Lee as early as the 1800s, as many of the Sunday's Well residents had boathouses at the bottom of their gardens.

The Cork Agricultural Exhibition was held on the Carrigrohane Road. It opened on 11 May 1932 and continued until 2 October. It covered thirteen acres, which accommodated agricultural and horticultural sections, flower beds, shrubberies and, of course, amusements. The large car park could hold in excess of 3,000 vehicles. Postcards were produced showing scenes from the exhibition, including the entrance (*above*) and an overview of the area (*below*).

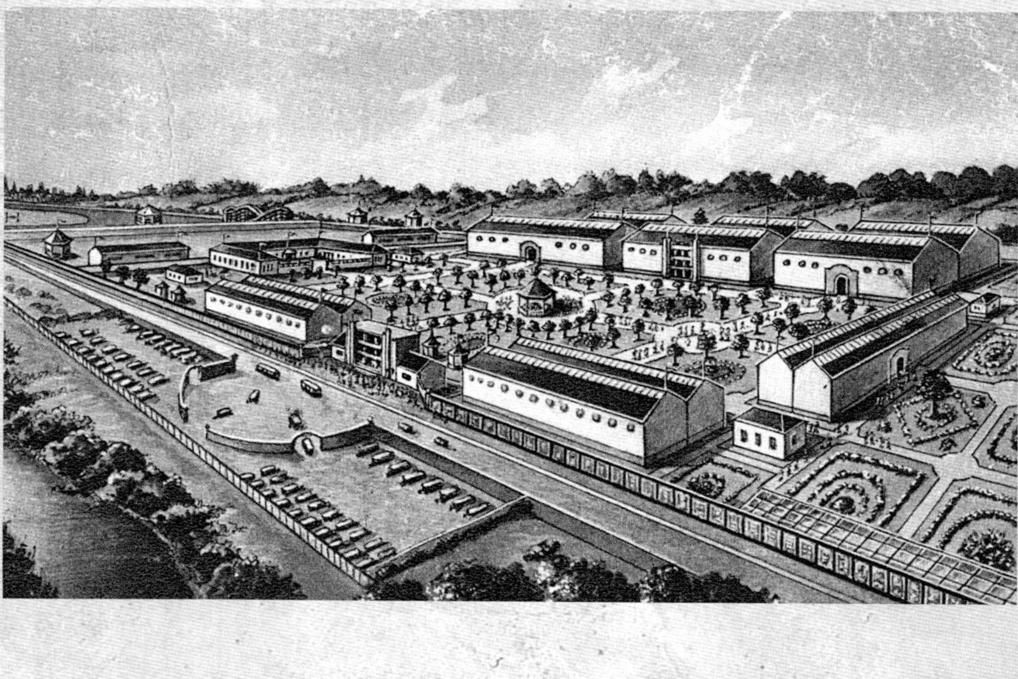

On the far side of the river the old Cork Waterworks have been on this site since the 1760s. The present building, renamed the Lifetime Lab and used as an educational facility, houses many wonderful pieces of Victorian engineering, such as huge coal-fired boilers, steam engines and water turbines. The beautiful red-brick structure is the best-preserved Victorian water pumping station in Ireland. In the background of the image is the former Our Lady's Hospital.

Heading back towards the city we reach Wellington Bridge, which was designed by the famous road surveyor Richard Griffith. It was constructed in 1830 following the lobbying of Cork's affluent Sunday's Well residents for access to the southern shore of the river. The nearest bridge to them at this point was the North Gate Bridge near the city centre. Wellington Bridge was named

in honour of the Duke of Wellington, whose successful campaign against Napoleon Bonaparte culminated in the Battle of Waterloo. The bridge was later officially renamed Thomas Davis Bridge, after the Young Irelander, but the old name of Wellington Bridge is still commonly used.

In this tranquil scene looking down-river before the construction of Daly's Bridge, a fishing boat is laying its nets on the River Lee. In olden days the river was so well stocked with eels, trout and salmon, that fishermen were able to earn a good living selling their produce to local fishmongers.

Two gentlemen gaze over the river near the old Ferry Quay in 1909, before Daly's Bridge was built. Prior to the building of the bridge a ferry used to carry passengers from here to the other side. The ferry operator was compensated for his loss of business when Cork's only suspension bridge was built.

Daly's Bridge is one of Cork's favourite bridges, colloquially known as the Shaky Bridge because of the way the suspension shakes when pedestrians are crossing. Due to the philanthropy of James Daly, a merchant and resident of Sunday's Well, the bridge was completed in 1927.

The Good Shepherd's Convent in Sunday's Well, on Convent Avenue, was designed by G. C. Ashlin in 1871 as an Industrial School and Magdalen Asylum for the reform of 'fallen' women. It was once home to the saintly child known as Little Nellie, whose grave is still on the site. Despite a preservation order, the building was badly damaged by fire and has subsequently been abandoned by commercial interests.

CORK — St. Vincents Church, Sundays Well.

St Vincent's Church is a famous of landmark of Sunday's Well and still a notable part of the Cork skyline. It was designed by Sir John Benson and was the home of the Vincentian Order. The church was built of red sandstone in the early Gothic style and was constructed in 1856. The Presbytery is now owned and used by the UCC School of Music.

An early Christmas card view of the Sunday's Well Road with St Vincent's on the left. The style of the card suggests that the image is older than the card itself. Behind the railings to the right of the image are the steps which lead up to Blair's Hill and Blarney Street.

A Cork Pictorial Card Company image of St Vincent's Bridge, which links Sunday's Well to the marsh area of the city near the Mercy Hospital. Although it lacks detail,

the image has an almost childlike charm. The original bridge in this location was constructed of timber, but the present steel pedestrian bridge was built in 1878.

The North Mall *c.* 1880, one of the city's most desirable addresses during the Georgian period. Many rich Cork merchants such as the Jennings and the Lanes chose to live there. An old wrought-iron arch still in existence at the entrance of one of these houses is a rare survivor from the Georgian period in Cork.

The North Mall was built on the site of an old Franciscan abbey. During the building of the present houses, stone coffins of great antiquity were uncovered. The area's history is recalled today in the name of the Franciscan Well Brewery. This image dates to *c.* 1910.

A very unusual view of the Mercy Hospital taken from Wise's Distillery. This photographic-quality postcard was issued by the Sisters of Mercy to raise funds for the hospital, which they founded in 1857.

The building that housed the Mercy Hospital was originally the mayor's house. The Mayoralty House was built by the celebrated Italian architect Davis Ducart, at the enormous expense of £3,793. It was started in 1767 and was not completed until 1773, when £69 8s 2d was paid for a small Doric feature around the entrance. Despite its new use, the building, with its original windows and cut limestone, retains its grand character.

Henry Street in the 1950s, showing an NSU garage. NSU was a German car manufacturer that was eventually acquired by Volkswagen. It is very unusual to obtain pictures of streets such as this, as many were privately taken by camera enthusiasts. (*Courtesy of Charlie Ginnane*)

The Lee Boot Manufacturing Company was located on the site of the present-day premises of Square Deal on Lancaster Quay. A huge range of quality leather shoes and boots were manufactured there – the annual output was 300,000

pairs. Such was the demand that thousands of pairs were exported to Britain and the firm employed over 350 workers. It closed in the 1980s because of competition from cheaper imported shoes.

COMBINE **STYLE, WEAR** AND **COMFORT**

98519.J.V.
WASH

This photograph of Washington Street in the 1920s shows the Sunday's Well tram and, to the right, a motorcycle and motor car of the period. The Washington public house, in the building behind the tram, was a Murphy's tied house (where the pub was under the control of a specific brewery), as can be seen from the advertising sign on the gable wall.

The Courthouse on Washington Street was erected in 1835 and was designed by the Pain brothers, James and George. This postcard by William Lawrence, *c.* 1905, shows the size and scale of the building. Note the railings, which were a common feature of notable Cork buildings. Their removal sometime in the mid twentieth century lessened the visual impact of the building.

ELEVATION TO G[illegible]

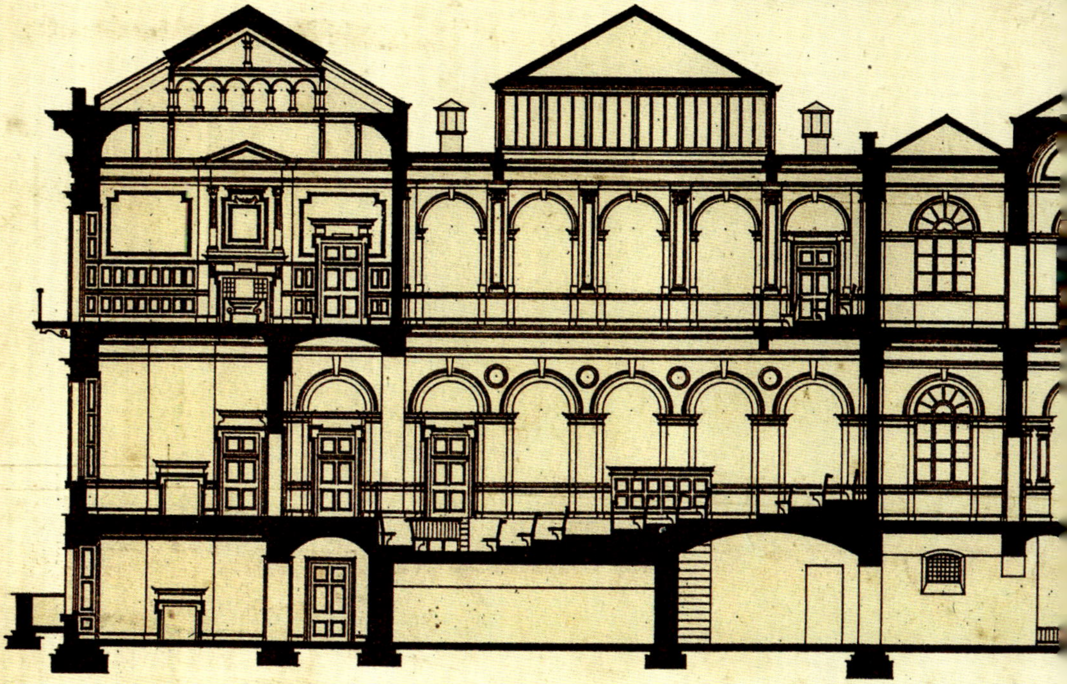

LONGITU

During Good Friday 1891, at the trial of five Tipperary men, a terrible fire engulfed the Courthouse. Subsequently a competition was held to redesign it. These sectional drawings were made by Sir Thomas Deane & Son for the

Cork Courthouse rebuilding competition. This was a very well executed design, which nevertheless proved unsuccessful.

The Cork architect William H. Hill was the successful candidate in the competition to redesign the Courthouse. The Hill family have a long association with

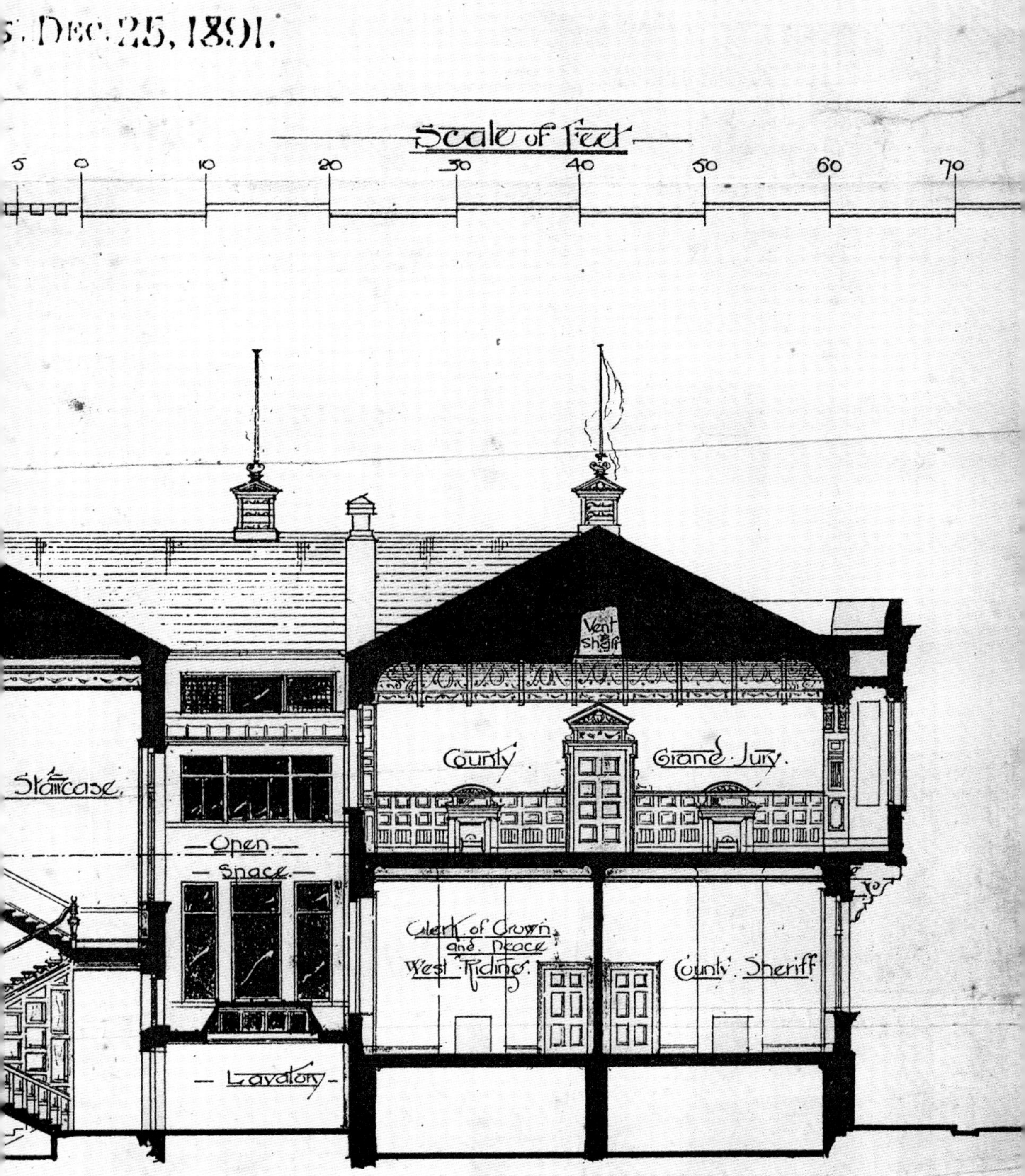

Cork architecture and were responsible for designing the Metropole Hotel and the Crawford School of Art and Design as well.

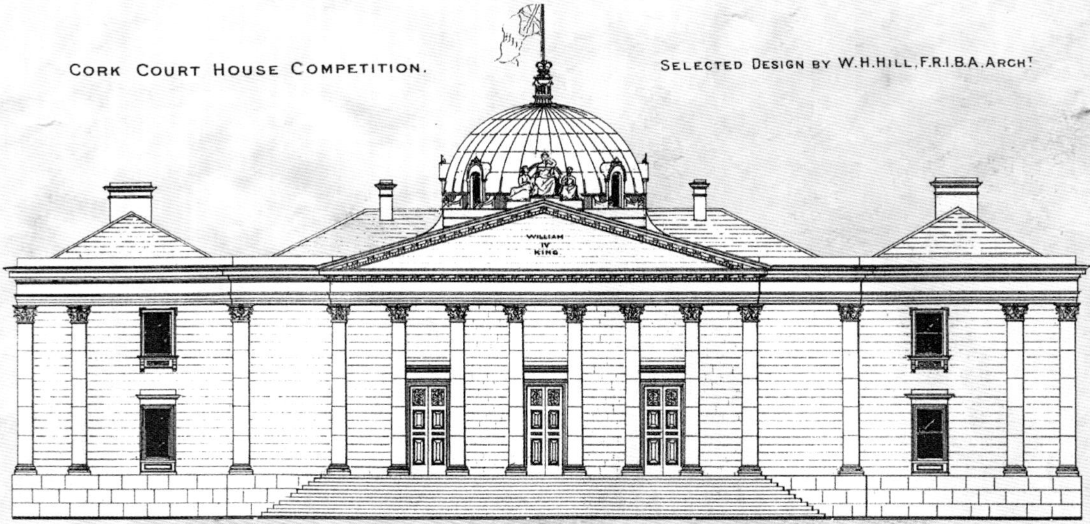

These drawings from the *Building News* of December 1891 give us an insight into the minute detail involved in the planning. The original portico of 1835 survived the fire and was incorporated into the new building.

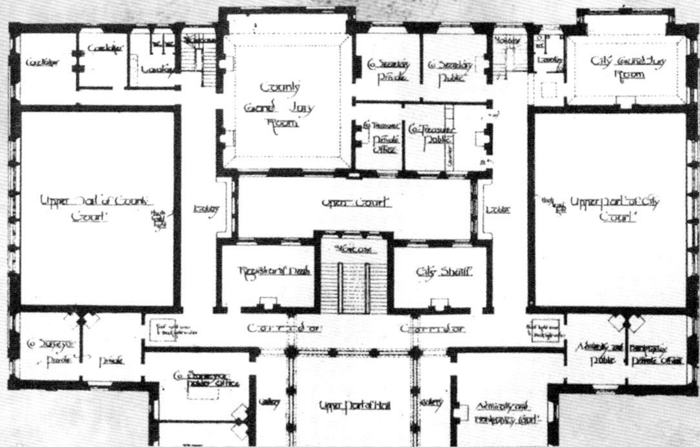

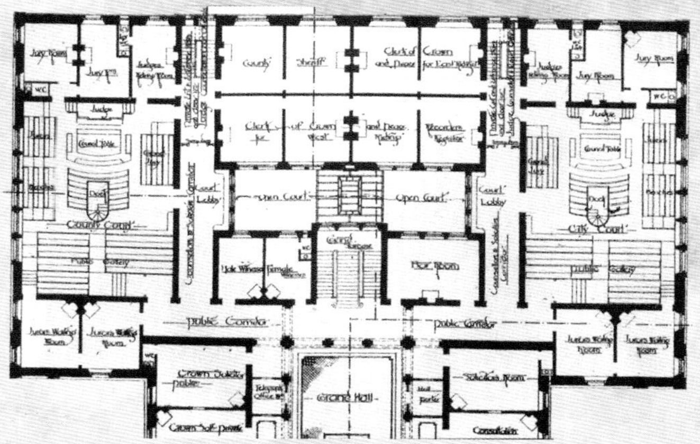

Two trams, numbers 18 and 13, travel in tandem, complete with their respective advertising boards. These trams brought passengers to the Mardyke and Sunday's Well from the city centre, along Washington Street, shown here. The sidecar to the left was another popular mode of transport.

The Dwyer family was one of Cork's great merchant families. This early twentieth-century advertisement shows their shop and showrooms (now Courthouse Chambers) built in 1874 on Great George's Street. The street was renamed Washington Street after the first president of the United States of America. The city council passed the motion renaming the street on 27 September 1918.

This photograph from the late 1920s shows a view of Washington Street heading out of the city centre. This Georgian street was specifically designed as the main gateway from the west into the city. The horses are well laden as they pull wagons filled to capacity in this busy street scene.

This is a wonderful view showing the wide expanse of the Grand Parade. Finn's Corner and Singer's Corner opposite each other are synonymous with the streetscape. Finn's was established in 1858 and Singer's has been there since 1875.

WHOLESALE & R
80
CLOTHING STO
SINGER
SEWING MACHINES

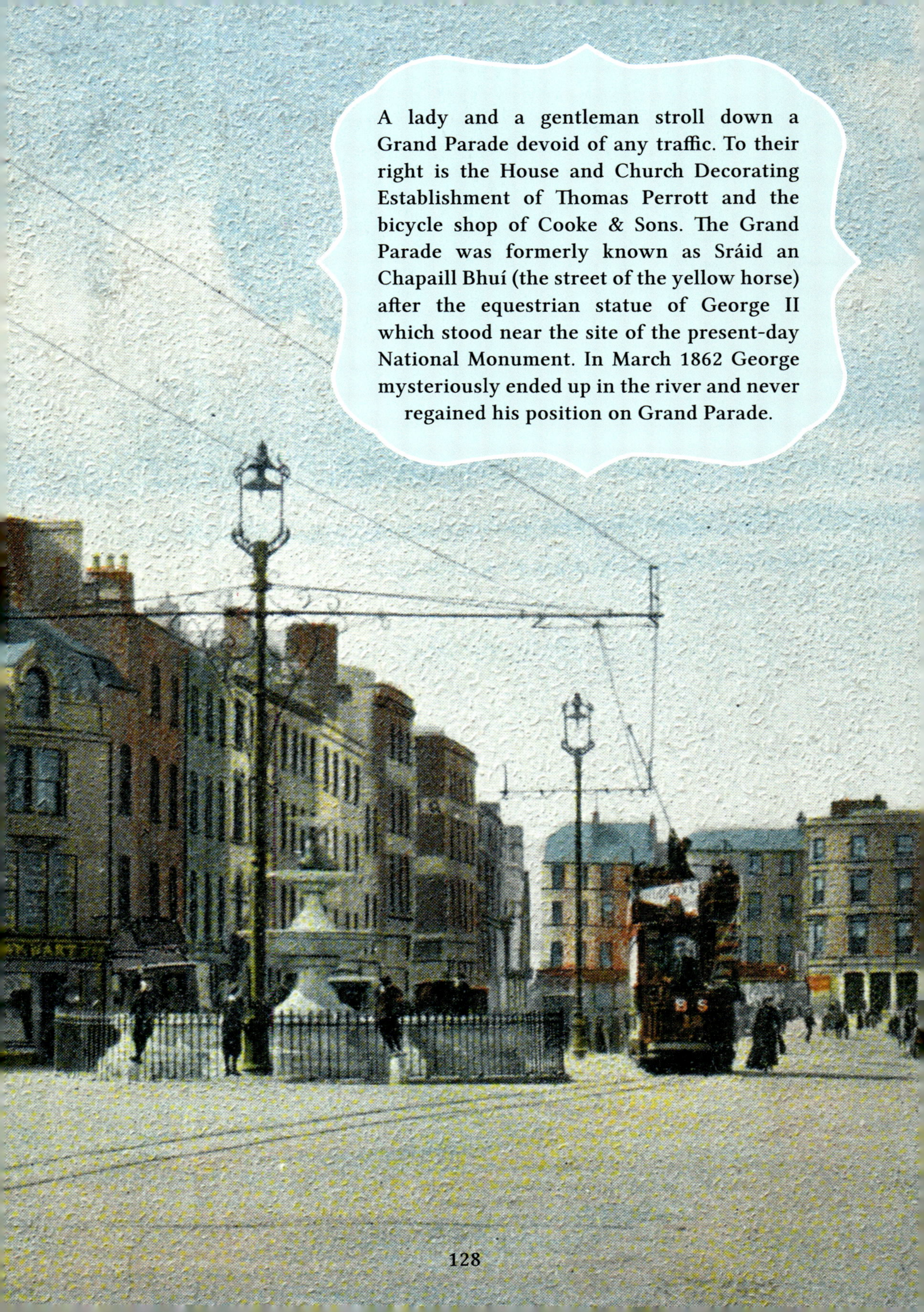

A lady and a gentleman stroll down a Grand Parade devoid of any traffic. To their right is the House and Church Decorating Establishment of Thomas Perrott and the bicycle shop of Cooke & Sons. The Grand Parade was formerly known as Sráid an Chapaill Bhuí (the street of the yellow horse) after the equestrian statue of George II which stood near the site of the present-day National Monument. In March 1862 George mysteriously ended up in the river and never regained his position on Grand Parade.

DECORATING
CYCLE
DEPÔT.
COOKE & SONS
CYCLES

The canopies outside these premises on the Grand Parade lend an almost continental air to the streetscape. Note the extremely old bow-fronted building on the right. J. C. Foley was a confectioner and also operated a post office from his premises at No. 9 Grand Parade. In 1908, around the time this picture was taken, Nos 1, 2 and 4 were vintners.

A young boy poses for a picture on the Grand Parade. This area was a busy hub for trams, as can be seen by the electric standards in this picture. In the background, behind the stationary tram, the Alexander Grant department store can be seen, which was destroyed by a fire in March 1942. Further along the street can be seen the ornate entrance to the famous English Market, which is still in use today.

The Cork Young Ireland Society was very much to the fore in organising funds for the erection of the National Monument on the Grand Parade, which was unveiled on St Patrick's Day 1906. It was constructed in memory of the men who fought for Irish freedom in the years 1798, 1803, 1848 and 1867. The foundation stone was laid during the centenary of the 1798 rebellion. It was to take a further eight years before it was completed.

A 1930s colour-tinted postcard of the Grand Parade, showing the completed National Monument. Various forms of transport including a brewery horse and dray, a bus and a bicycle encompass the different conveyances of the day.

This scene from the 1950s clearly shows that cars were becoming more common. The number of cars parked all the way along the street also demonstrates that this area was at the commercial heart of the city.

No remains of the trams are evident in this view; all the tram lines and standards have been removed. The arrival of the bus had sounded the death knell for the trams in 1931. Various bus companies existed in the city until the routes were monopolised by CIÉ, which was founded in 1945.

This photograph of the South Mall, also from the 1950s, shows a Leyland bus in the foreground and to the right No. 41 South Mall. It is now home to the Electric Bar and Restaurant.

The South Mall has always been at the professional and commercial heart of the city. The legal profession, banks, stockbrokers and auctioneers have their businesses there. Many of Cork's finest stone and brick buildings are on this street, demonstrating the opulence of the area in the eighteenth and nineteenth centuries.

A picture of the Munster & Leinster Bank, 66 South Mall. The bank was established in 1885 following the collapse of the Munster Bank. James J. Murphy, the brewer, came to the rescue and established the Munster & Leinster Bank, a case of a Cork brewery saving a bank from extinction. This beautiful building was built by the Cork builders, Sisk & Company, and was completed in 1914.

LEINSTER

The two banking institutions of the National Bank (top) and Bank of Ireland, which were both located on the South Mall.

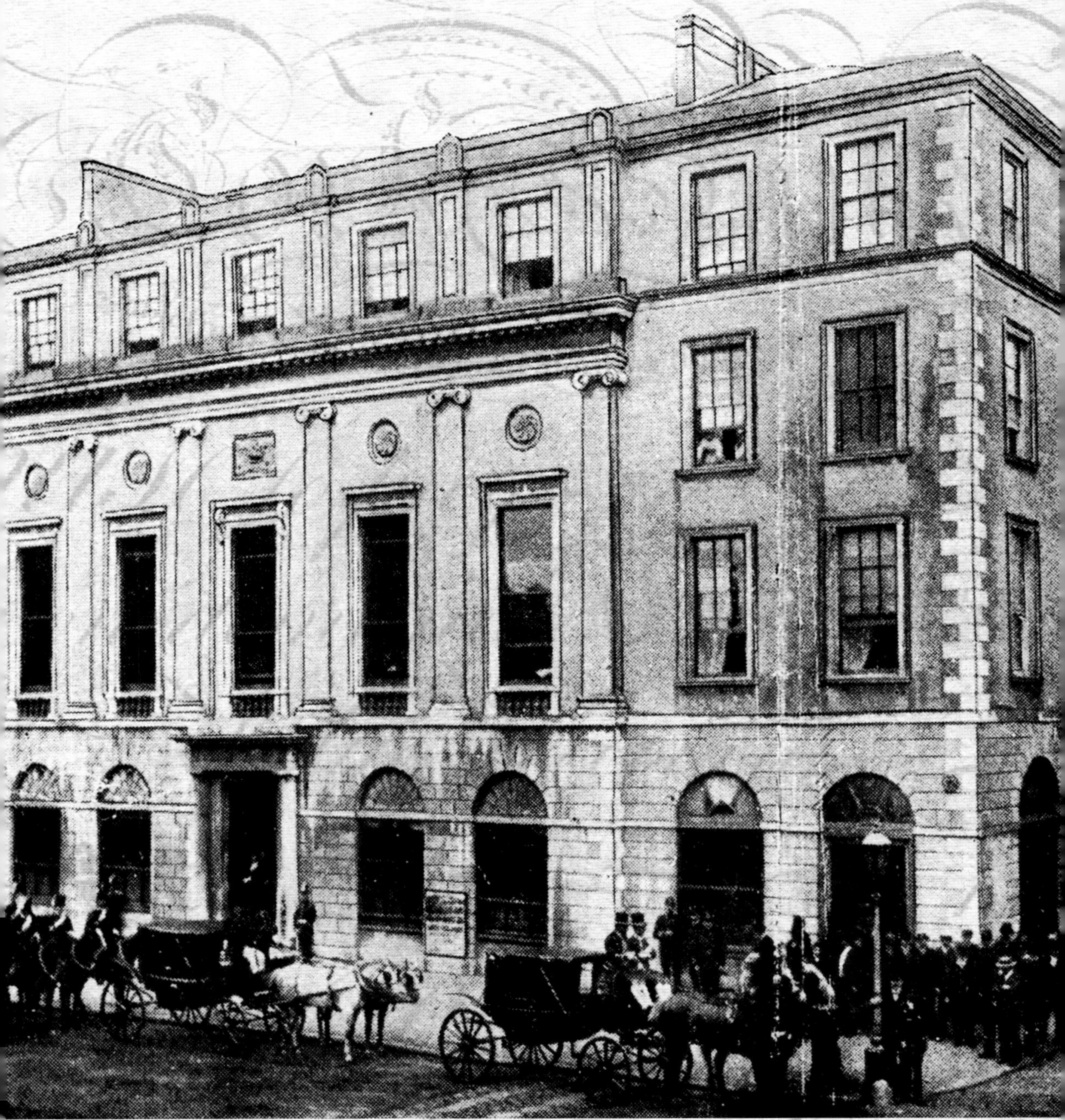

The Imperial Hotel, which incorporated the Commercial Buildings, was built in 1819 to cater to the members of the Commercial Buildings Company, including overseas visitors. The company was formed by a group of merchants in Cork to encourage trade and the building included a hotel and commercial rooms. The hotel was leased to a Mr Joyce at a rent of £700 over a seven-year period and it was originally named the Imperial Clarence Hotel. The external character of the building has changed since Thomas Deane designed it as one of the first great buildings on the South Mall.

The original Post Office, shown here, was located on Pembroke Street, just off the South Mall. This was later to become the initial site of the Cork Savings Bank. Since 1877 the GPO has been located on the site of the old Theatre Royal. *Inset:* A rare survivor: an original Post Office Deposit Book belonging to George Morris of 4 Alta Place, St Luke's. The first deposit was made in 1904.

A Lawrence view of an electric tram passing the old Provincial Bank towards the end of the South Mall. This is still one of Cork's most beautiful buildings. It was designed by the architect William G. Murray and completed in 1867.

This very old and extremely rare photograph of a busy quayside scene on the South Mall was taken around 1870, before the building of the Sutton's premises. It is hard to imagine looking at today's city that sailing ships would come this far upriver to dock and discharge their cargoes.

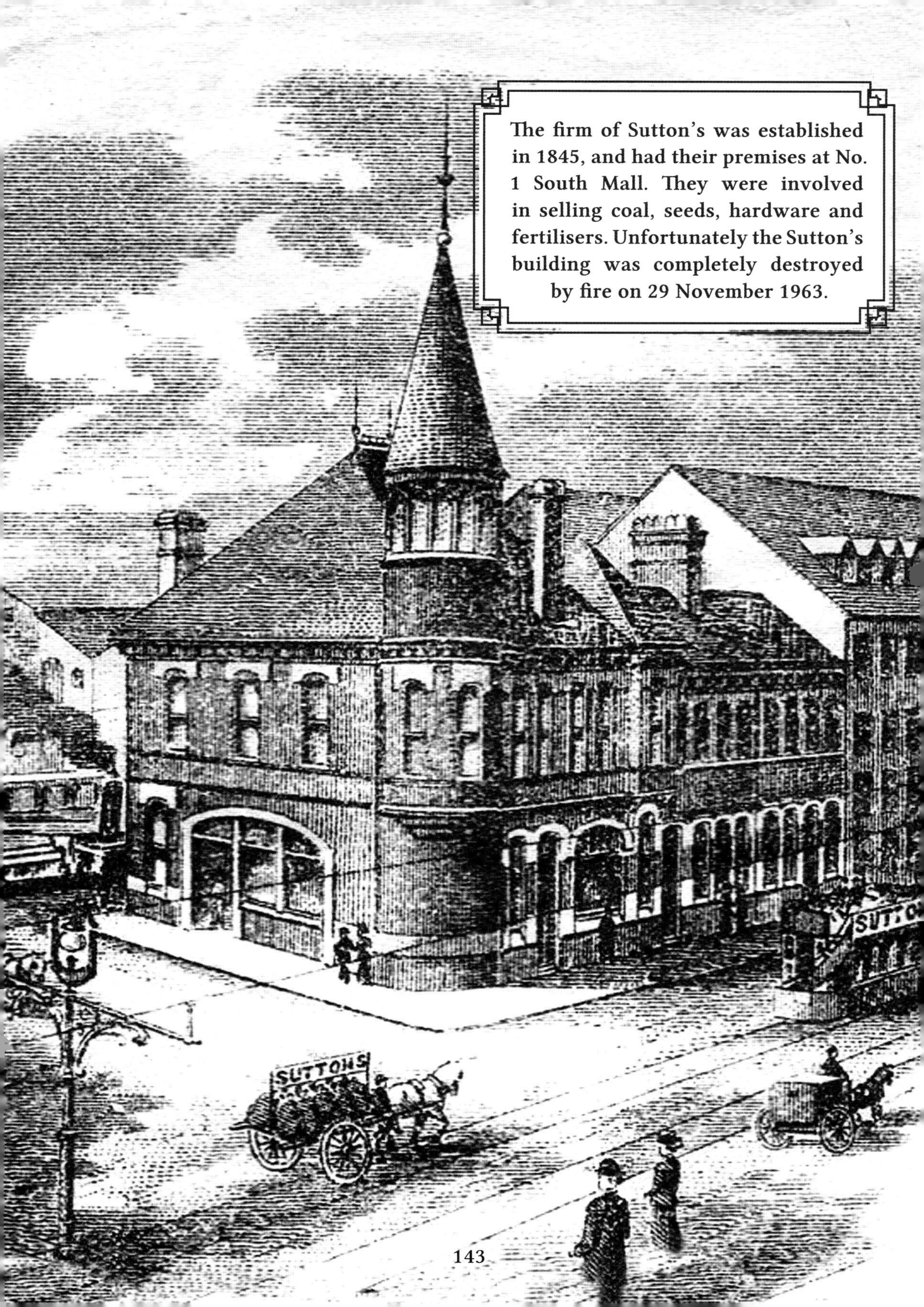

The firm of Sutton's was established in 1845, and had their premises at No. 1 South Mall. They were involved in selling coal, seeds, hardware and fertilisers. Unfortunately the Sutton's building was completely destroyed by fire on 29 November 1963.

AKED BEANS
ORSE RADISH

The old City Hall and, to its right, the Carnegie Library, seen from the end of the South Mall *c.* 1910. The library was designed by Henry A. Cutler and built in 1905, but was destroyed by crown forces in December 1920, during the burning of Cork. The City Hall was also destroyed during this conflagration. The tram in the foreground has just crossed over the old Parnell Swing Bridge.

This Gruss Aus-type postcard shows George's Street (now Oliver Plunkett Street) in the late 1890s. Turners Hotel was at No. 64, which was near Grafton's Alley. These late Victorian cards were sketched to almost photographic quality, as photographs themselves were costly to reproduce.

Messrs Porte & Co., located on George's Street, was one of the earliest electrical engineering firms in Cork. Porte & Co. was the sole contractor for the 1902/03 Cork International Exhibitions, providing lighting for 200 arc lamps and thousands of incandescent lamps.

The old Theatre Royal, designed by Sir John Benson, caught fire in the 1860s and never reopened as a theatre. Instead, using the surviving façade, the building was redesigned and opened as the current GPO in 1877.

CORK—BALLYCOTTON

CIÉ's omnibus department on Parnell Place is seen here with a single-decker Leyland bus stationed outside. The present CIÉ bus station was designed by Mary Fitzgibbon and J. R. Boyd-Barrett and built between the years 1958 and 1960.

leave Cork at 2.30 p.m.

Irish Omnibus Co. Ltd.,

40, 41, GRAND PARADE, CORK.

ne Cork 1435.

HOUSTON, CORK

Merchant's Quay, but certainly not as we know it now. When this photograph was taken, *c.* 1900, this quay was a hive of activity, with hotels, public houses, insurance companies and shipping agents trading along it. The higgledy-piggledy buildings had a certain charm, unlike the massive brick structure that exists today.

A paddle steamer at the top of Merchant's Quay adjoining St Patrick's Bridge in the 1880s. People and horse-drawn vehicles are evident in this busy quayside scene. This maritime area was home to ship chandlers, rope makers and the Cork Sailors' Home.

A later image of the same area, which dates to the 1940s, shows the differences that developed over the course of half a century in Cork. Horse-drawn transport has been replaced by horsepower.

An electric tram complete with an Alcock's tea advertising board crossing St Patrick's Bridge from the Merchant's Quay side. Advertising signs were a useful way for the tram company to generate revenue. In the background the green

fields had not yet succumbed to the massive building projects of Gurranabraher and its surrounding areas.

CIÉ buses feature predominantly in this black and white view of St Patrick's Bridge. The building on the corner of St Patrick's Street and Merchant's Quay was for years home to the Cork Gas Consumers' Company, which was established in 1860 by an Act of Parliament.

An original black and white photograph from the 1920s showing a tram and horse-drawn vehicles on St Patrick's Bridge.

When CIÉ was formed in 1945 it quickly gained a monopoly over the city's bus service. Smaller bus companies, such as the Irish Omnibus Company, which ran buses like those seen in this picture, closed as their routes were subsumed by CIÉ. To the right of this image is the famous Swan & Cygnet pub and the Dainty Restaurant.

DAINTY RESTAURANT
GUINNESS IS GOOD FOR YOU

A similar scene of the bridge, but this one is unusual in that it shows the bridge at night. When this postcard was created in 1904, photography had not yet advanced to such a stage as to produce a night-time scene. This did not deter the publishers from taking a daytime picture and manipulating it to produce this 'moonlit' image.

St. Patrick's Bridge

Father Mathew Statue, Cork.

Fr Mathew, the Apostle of Temperance, still stands guard over the city at the top of St Patrick's Street. This statue, by John Foley, has stood here since 1867. For many years the statue was the official destination for CIÉ buses at the top of St Patrick's Street – one wonders how tourists knew where the bus marked 'Statue' would bring them!

Right: One of Cork's early trams, with Drawbridge Street to its right.

F.W.RUSSELL
TEA & WINE
IMPORTER
117
H. BUCKLE
WHITEHAVEN
COALS
AGENT
E.D.WRIXON.
W S
12
F.W.RUSSELL
TWO SHILLINGS
119

A busy St Patrick's Street scene *c.* 1890, complete with resplendent carriages. The main commercial thoroughfare of the city was frequented by well-dressed ladies and gentlemen.

80, PATRICK STREET

Mechanised transport was the order of the day in this view from the 1920s. At this time motor cars were the prerequisite of the rich, yet, from the evidence of this photograph, Cork seems to have had its fair share.

An American stereo view of a busy St Patrick's Street, showing the hustle and bustle of city life. On the left an extremely large wagon makes its way down the street. The ornate gas lamps outside Cash & Company are sadly no longer extant.

An unusual view of St Patrick's Street, with pigs crossing the main thoroughfare. Many of the city's slaughterhouses were located on the north side of the city, in Blackpool and Cattle Market Street. Pork was big business and the firm of Lunham's was dispatching 180 pigs per hour in 1892 to cope with demand from their London agency.

This scene of St Patrick's Street between Winthrop Street and Maylor Street after the burning in 1920 shows what a desolate empty void was left behind. Miraculously the old Lee Cinema on Winthrop Street, on the extreme right of the picture, survived the conflagration. London House, the department store which was owned by William Roche, was another fine building put to the torch. Some businesses, such as the Lee Boot Company and Scully & O'Connells, were never to reopen after the fire.

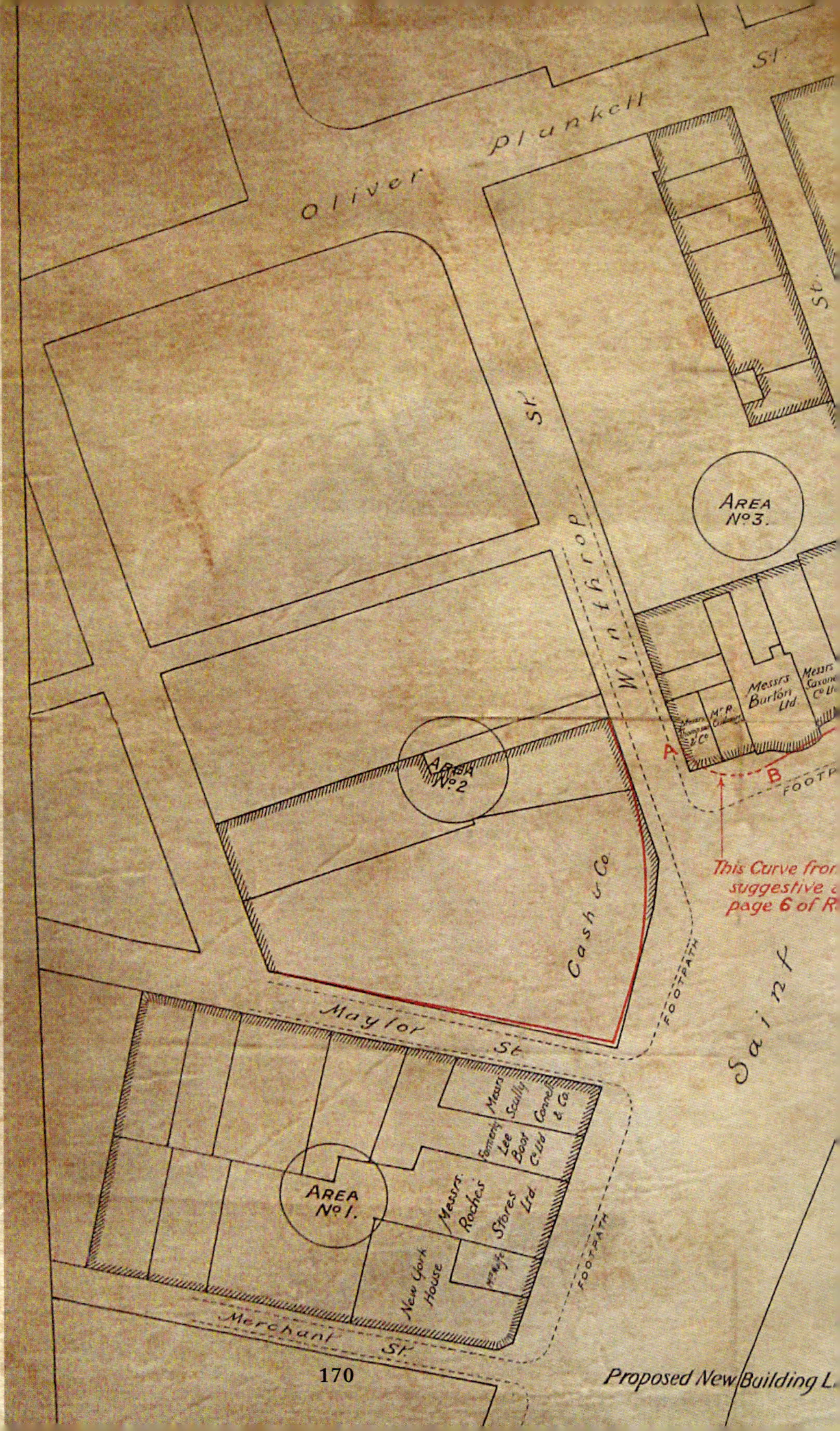

Oliver Plunkett St.
St.
Winthrop St.
AREA No 3.
Messrs Burton Ltd.
A
B
FOOTPATH
This Curve fron
suggestive
page 6 of R
AREA No 2.
Cash & Co
Maylor St
Saint
Messrs Scully
Connell & Co
Formerly Lee Boot Co Ltd
AREA No 1.
Messrs. Roches Stores Ltd
New York House
Merchant St
Proposed New Building L

A plan showing the new building lines proposed for St Patrick's Street after the burning of Cork city in 1920. It is interesting to note the position of the old premises in relation to their current location today. The detail of the premises destroyed is extensive and shows their exact location before the fire. Many of these premises never reopened despite receiving compensation from the British Government as part of the Treaty negotiations, and new businesses took their place.

People stare in disbelief at the commercial heart of the city that was burned to the ground by British forces. This image shows the remains of Sunner's Chemist on St Patrick's Street. Thousands of workers became unemployed because of this mindless act of vandalism.

Above and overleaf: Photographs of the funeral of Terence MacSwiney passing Nos 74–75 St Patrick's Street, the premises of Alcock's Teas. This was one of the largest republican funerals ever to take place and was the visible outpouring of grief and anger over the death of Cork's Lord Mayor, who had spent seventy-four days on hunger strike in Brixton Prison.

74 ALCOCK 75
ALCOCK'S
DELICIOUS
TEAS
PRODUCE MERCHANT
TEA IMPORTER

One of Cork's oldest shops, Cash & Company, started life as Todd & Company, established in 1834, and later became Carmichael's Department Store, before being taken over by Cash's. Cash is actually an anagram which stands for Carmichael, Arnott and McOstrich, who were the directors. Now the home of Brown Thomas, it is still providing a rich heritage of quality and service.

Bot. of Woodford, Bourne & Co. Ltd
Grocers and Wine Merchants.
By Appointment to His Majesty the King.

At the other end of St Patrick's Street is another iconic building. The grocery firm of Woodford, Bourne & Co., Nos 64–65 St Patrick's Street, was originally established as early as 1750, when it was Rooke & Company. This wonderful building is one of the oldest on the street and is an integral part of the streetscape.

"	Double Diamond	10. 9.	12 X ½ pts.	Guinness
"	Time	10. 0.	6 X ½ "	Cider
		2. 8. 6.	6 bots.	Club Orange

COAL QUAY MARKET AND

The old market on Coal Quay (Cornmarket Street) was an open market where country people sold their wares and so was commonly known as Paddy's Market. In the background is the old Bridewell, which was destroyed by anti-Treaty soldiers during the Civil War in August 1922.

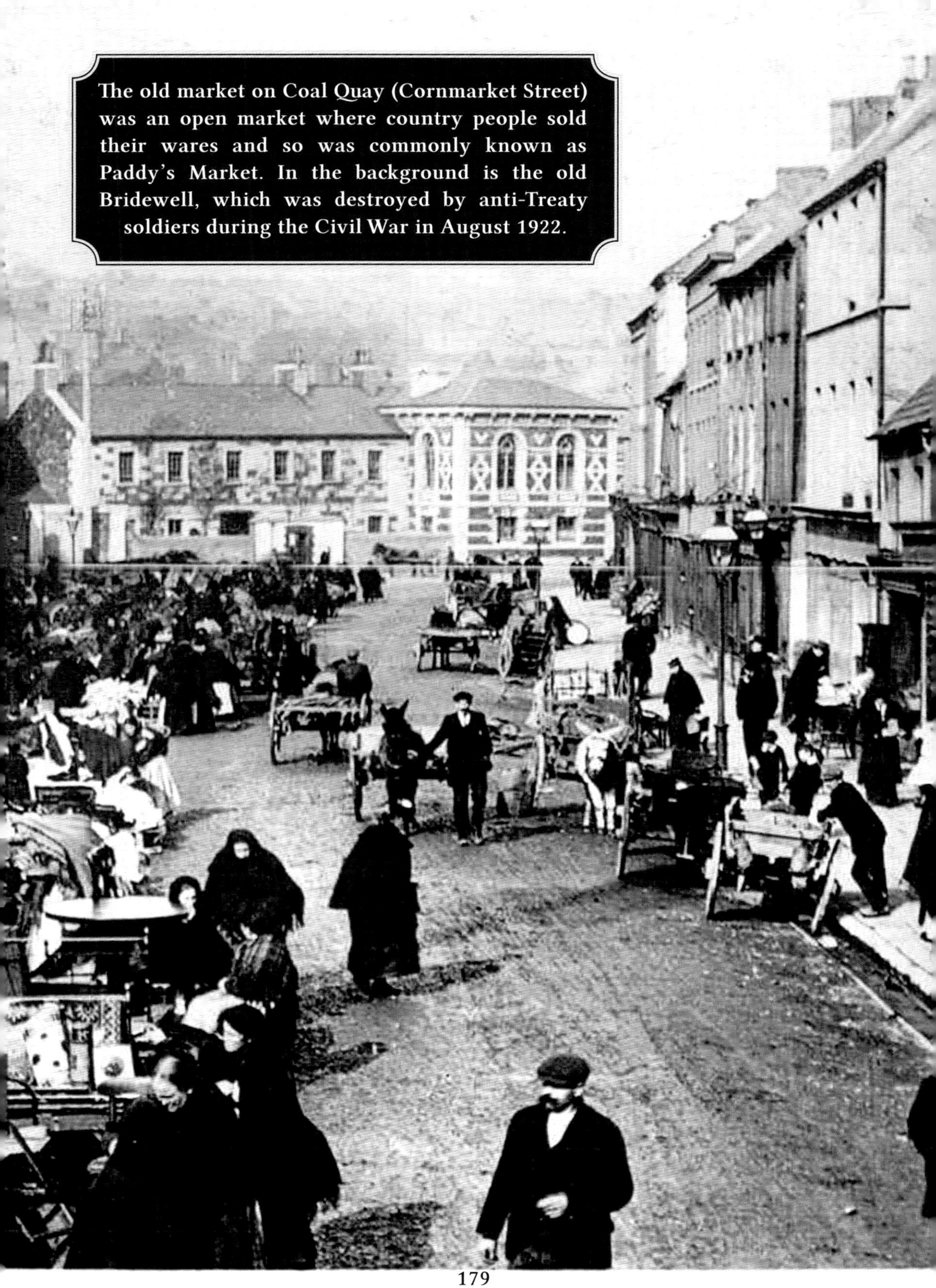

POLICE COURT, CORK.

A posed street scene on the Coal Quay taken by the American stereo view company of B. W. Kilburn, dated 1891. The boys in the photograph deployed the donkey and cart to transport heavy goods locally. This enabled them to earn a little money to supplement their family's meagre earnings and keep them on the breadline.

6392. Street Market, Cork, Ireland.

Paul's Avenue was named after St Paul's Church, which was erected in 1723. It was formerly known as Harper's Lane, after one of the city's merchant princes. This area housed many tenement buildings which were cleared in the late 1930s.

This photograph dates from the 1930s, when the old stocks still existed outside St Paul's Church in Paul Street. The man in the photograph is historian Philip G. Lee, who is sitting on the steps of the church. Following its deconsecration in 1950, Guy & Co. used the church building as a warehouse, up until 1997. It is now used by Fifty Degrees North.

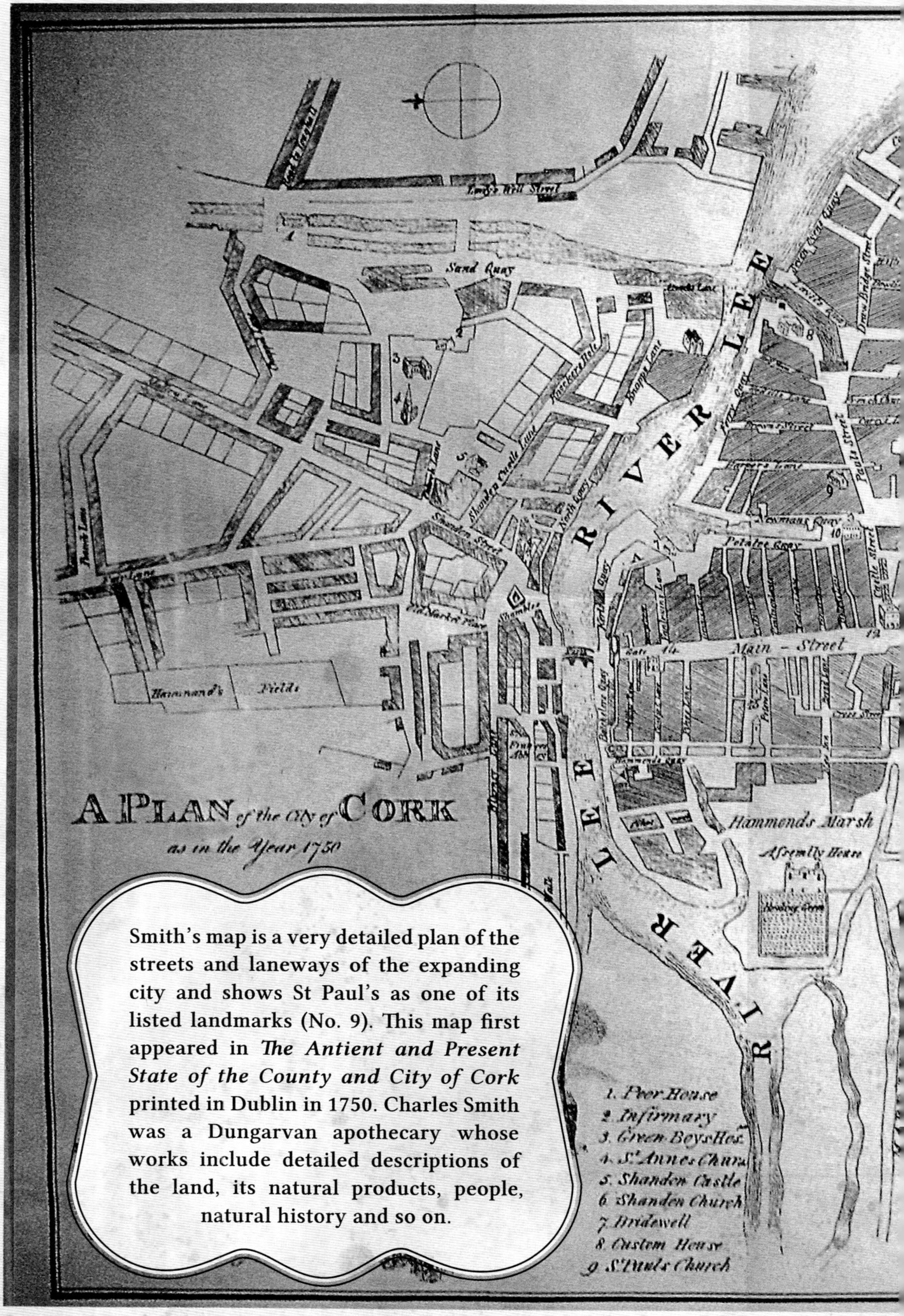

Smith's map is a very detailed plan of the streets and laneways of the expanding city and shows St Paul's as one of its listed landmarks (No. 9). This map first appeared in *The Antient and Present State of the County and City of Cork* printed in Dublin in 1750. Charles Smith was a Dungarvan apothecary whose works include detailed descriptions of the land, its natural products, people, natural history and so on.

VIII
SOUTH CHANNEL
Reap Marsh
About this Place the Duke of Grafton was Killed
Gabbett's Quay
Georges Street
Hoar's Quay
Duncomb's
Marsh
Mall
Post Office Quay
Fulham's Quay
Cove Lane
Red Abbey Lane
Friars Walk
Red Road
To Black Rock
Stephen's Hospital
Grave Yard Lane
Cut Lane
Street, South Gate
Fort
West
Marsh
To Gill Abbey
PARISHES.
St. Finn Barrs
Christ Church
St. Peters
St. Marys Shandon
St. Anne's
St. Pauls
New Corn Mark
County Court House
Exchange
St. Peter's Church
Skyddys Castle
Christ Church
Free School
Cathedral of St. Barrs
Draw Bridge
A B C D City Wall
Scale of 440 Yards 2 Furlongs or ¼ of a Mile

S. S. Peter and Paul's Church, Cork.

An unusual view of the Church of Ss Peter & Paul. Due to the close proximity of other buildings it is difficult today to obtain a good image of this church. Archdeacon John Murphy, of the family of brewers, was the primary force behind the building of this church. The foundation stone was laid on 15 August 1859 and the church was dedicated for worship on 29 June 1866.

S. S. Peter and Paul's Church, Cork.

This old stereo view shows the interior of the Gothic Revival church, which was designed by Augustus Pugin. It replaced the old chapel at Carey's Lane, which would have been extremely small, and celebrated its 150th anniversary in 2009.

School of Art & Opera House,

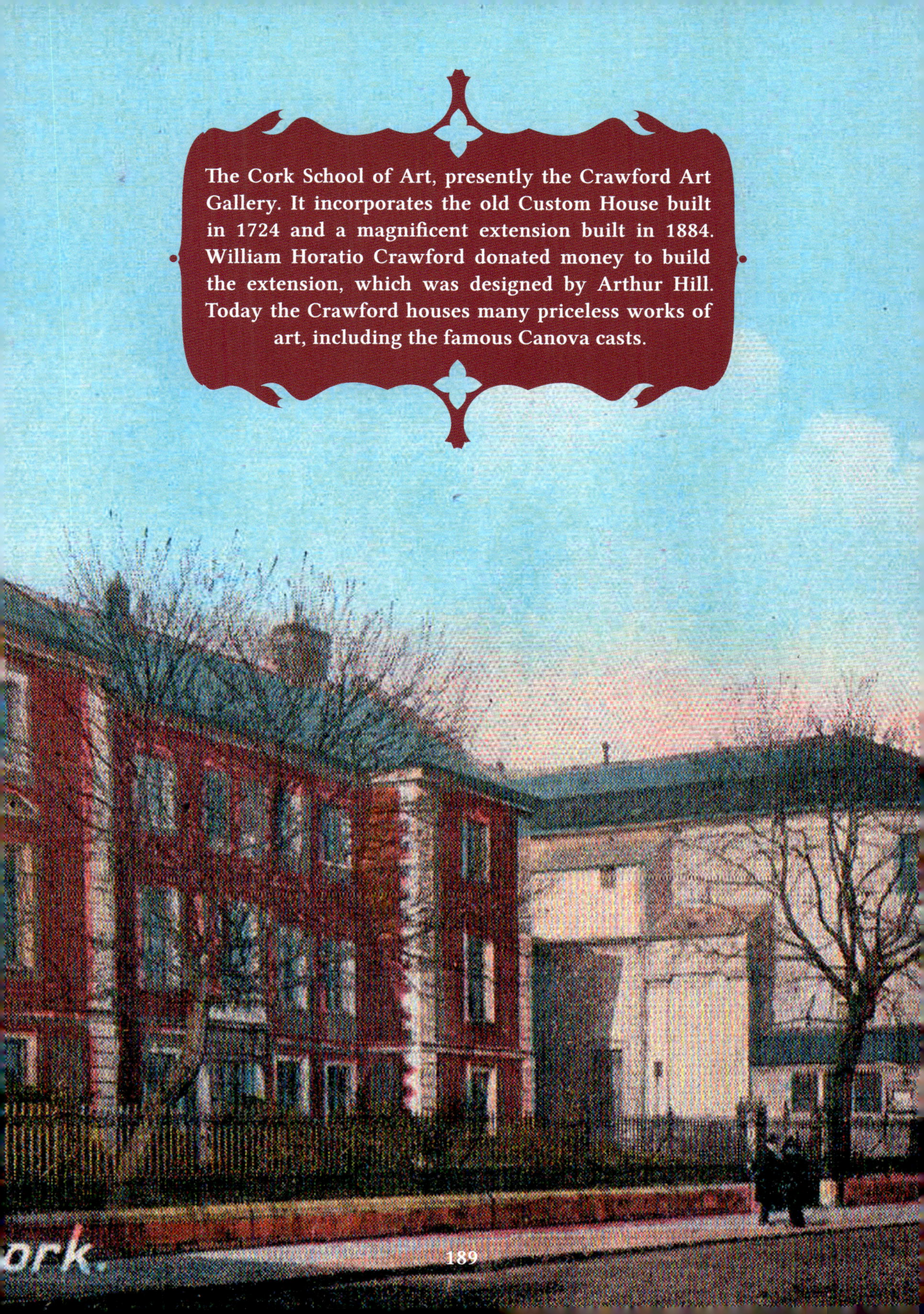

The Cork School of Art, presently the Crawford Art Gallery. It incorporates the old Custom House built in 1724 and a magnificent extension built in 1884. William Horatio Crawford donated money to build the extension, which was designed by Arthur Hill. Today the Crawford houses many priceless works of art, including the famous Canova casts.

This sketch by the artist R. L. Stopford shows what later became the first Cork Opera House, shortly after its erection in 1855 when it was the main concert hall in the city. Originally part of the Athenaeum, its opening was a huge occasion and the Lord Lieutenant, the Earl of Bandon, the Mayor and a host of other dignitaries arrived for the inauguration. Sailing boats could deliver patrons to the concert hall directly from the Lee.

The morning after the great conflagration, started by an electrical fault, that signalled the demise of the old Opera House in December 1955. To the right of the image can be seen the stage entrance at the top of Half Moon Street. The *Echo/ Examiner* stores which were also on this street contained a huge amount of paper rolls and if these had caught fire it would have decimated a large area. Thankfully, the fire brigade managed to control the blaze and prevent it from spreading.

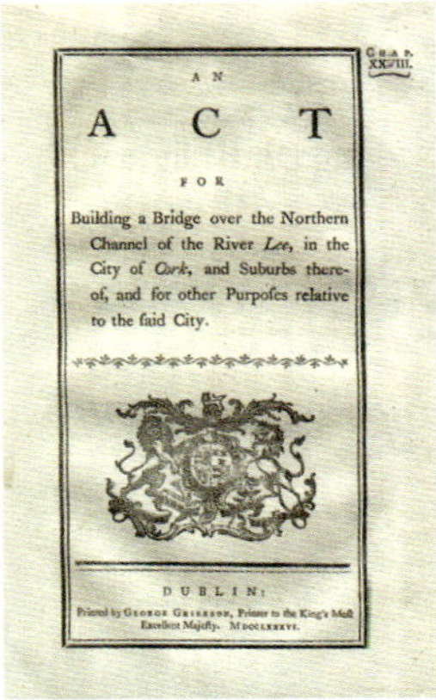

CHAP. XXVIII.

AN

ACT

FOR

Building a Bridge over the Northern Channel of the River *Lee*, in the City of *Cork*, and Suburbs thereof, and for other Purposes relative to the said City.

DUBLIN:

Printed by GEORGE GRIERSON, Printer to the King's Most Excellent Majesty. MDCCLXXXVI.

A busy St Patrick's Bridge scene looking towards Bridge Street from a postcard dating to *c.* 1905. The Act of Parliament (*inset*) to enable the building of St Patrick's Bridge was passed in 1786. The original bridge was a toll bridge. For a coach drawn by two horses or mules, the charge was 3d to cross. The old bridge was toll free by 1812. The present St Patrick's Bridge was declared officially open by Sir John Arnott on 12 December 1861.

A busy Bridge Street scene *c.* 1910. To the left is the well-known landmark of Barriscale's clock. The Cork firm of William Barriscale sold quality watches, clocks and jewellery from this premises to its many clients from 1893 to the mid twentieth century.

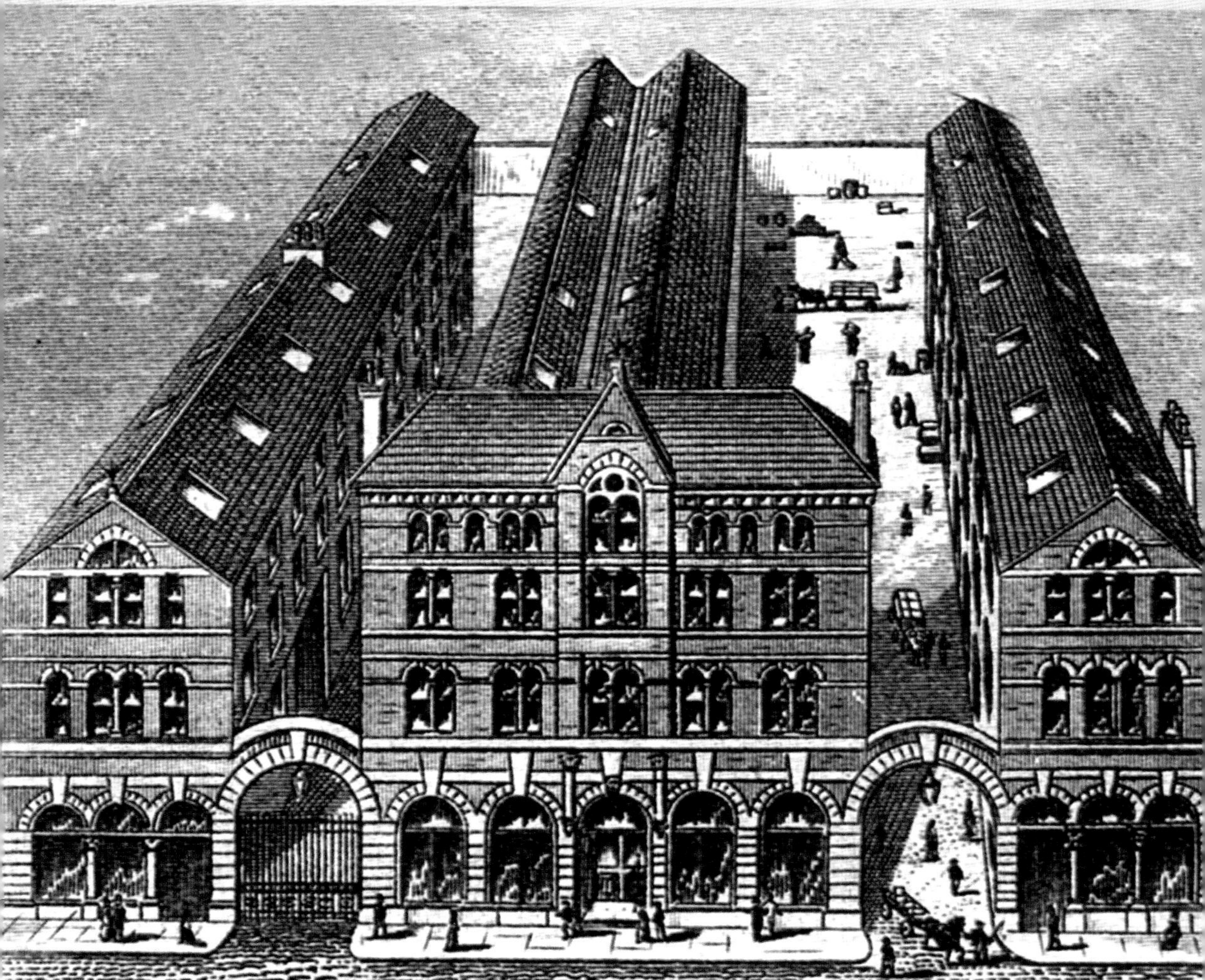

In 1883 the Hibernian Buildings on King Street (now MacCurtain Street) suffered a major blow when the premises of Dobbin & Ogilvie, a confectionary firm, caught fire. This conflagration prevented the firm from exhibiting at the Cork Exhibition of that year.

KING STREET, CORK.

'Phone 731.

MacCu

A wonderful view of MacCurtain Street showing Woollam's shop front and the Hibernian Buildings. These were similar in design to the Metropole Hotel on the opposite side of the street with its red-bricked, white-detailed, ornate turrets. This hotel was designed by Arthur Hill in 1897.

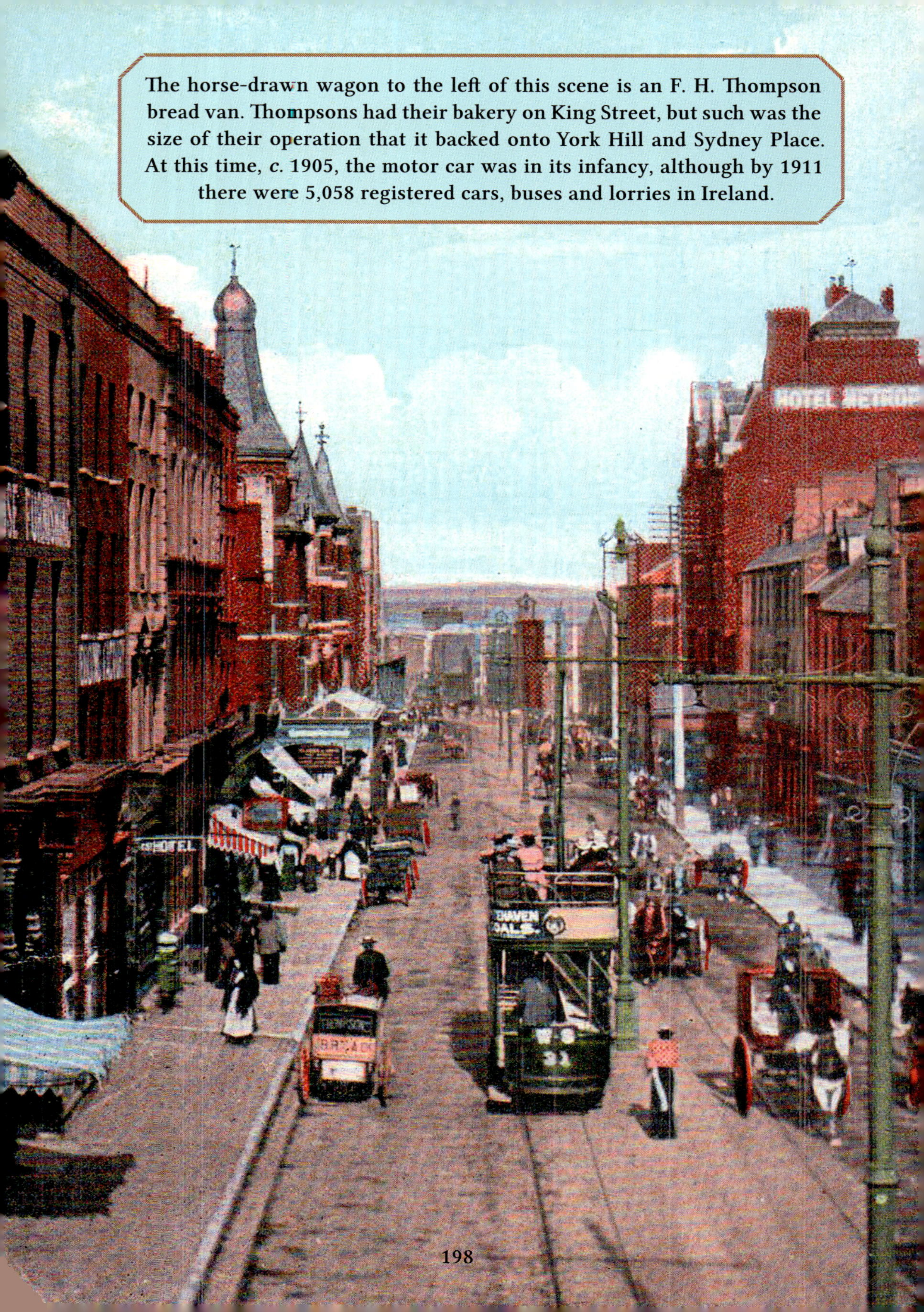

The horse-drawn wagon to the left of this scene is an F. H. Thompson bread van. Thompsons had their bakery on King Street, but such was the size of their operation that it backed onto York Hill and Sydney Place. At this time, *c.* 1905, the motor car was in its infancy, although by 1911 there were 5,058 registered cars, buses and lorries in Ireland.

Harutun Batmazian was an Armenian Christian who fled religious persecution in Constantinople. He arrived in Cork during the 1902 exhibition. There his Turkish Delight sold so well that he opened a sweet shop on MacCurtain Street. The shop was a virtual Aladdin's cave of sweets. The Hadji Bey brand quickly became popular with generations of Corkonians and the famous Turkish Delight is still available today.

PALACE
PALACE
THEATRE, CORK, LIMITED.
Manager - - Mr. THOS. F. O'BRIEN.
.50--TWICE NIGHTLY--9
MONDAY, 6th MAY, 1912
AND DURING THE WEEK.
cial and Important Engagement and First Appearance in Ireland of The
TWO
VIVIANS
America's Greatest Sharpshooters.

King Street was renamed MacCurtain Street in honour of the Cork patriot and Lord Mayor Tomás MacCurtain, who was murdered by British forces in March 1920. Strangely enough the members of the RIC who committed this crime were stationed in King Street. In 1897 Dan Lowrey established the Palace of Varieties, a new music hall, on the street. It often showed a series of short films known as the Palascope. By 1930 the Palace had become a full-time picture house. It now houses the Everyman Theatre.

The Presbyterian Trinity Church at the bottom of Summerhill, designed by the architect Colin Tarring, was completed in 1861. There is a distinctive kink in the spire of the church and it is said that the workmen did this deliberately due to non-payment of their wages. A myth also arose that the architect hanged himself in the tower, although thankfully there is no truth in this.

St Patrick's Church on the Lower Glanmire Road was designed by the architect George Pain and consecrated on 15 October 1859. The ornate portico is supported by six Corinthian columns. John Benson designed an extension in 1873.

These scenes show the arrival of William O'Brien on the Lower Glanmire Road in 1911. O'Brien, originally from Mallow, had founded the All-for-Ireland League in 1910 to oppose partition of Ireland and Home Rule, and it won eight seats in that

year's general election. O'Brien himself won a seat in Cork city. In these scenes throngs of supporters arrive from the nearby Great Southern & Western Railway. St Patrick's Church and the Metropole Laundry can be seen in the background.

REAT SOUTHERN RAILWAYS

The Great Southern and Western Railway on the Lower Glanmire Road. Then called Glanmire Station, its name was changed to Kent Station in 1966. The main-line terminus was opened on 1 February 1893 at a cost of £60,000. The new station was packed with sightseers for several days and for years afterwards it was known as 'the new station'. Unfortunately the 1970s saw the demise of the Youghal route, which had been a very popular destination for holidaymakers.

UNE, JULY, AUGUST and SEPTEMBER

CORK DISTRICT.

HALF-DAY

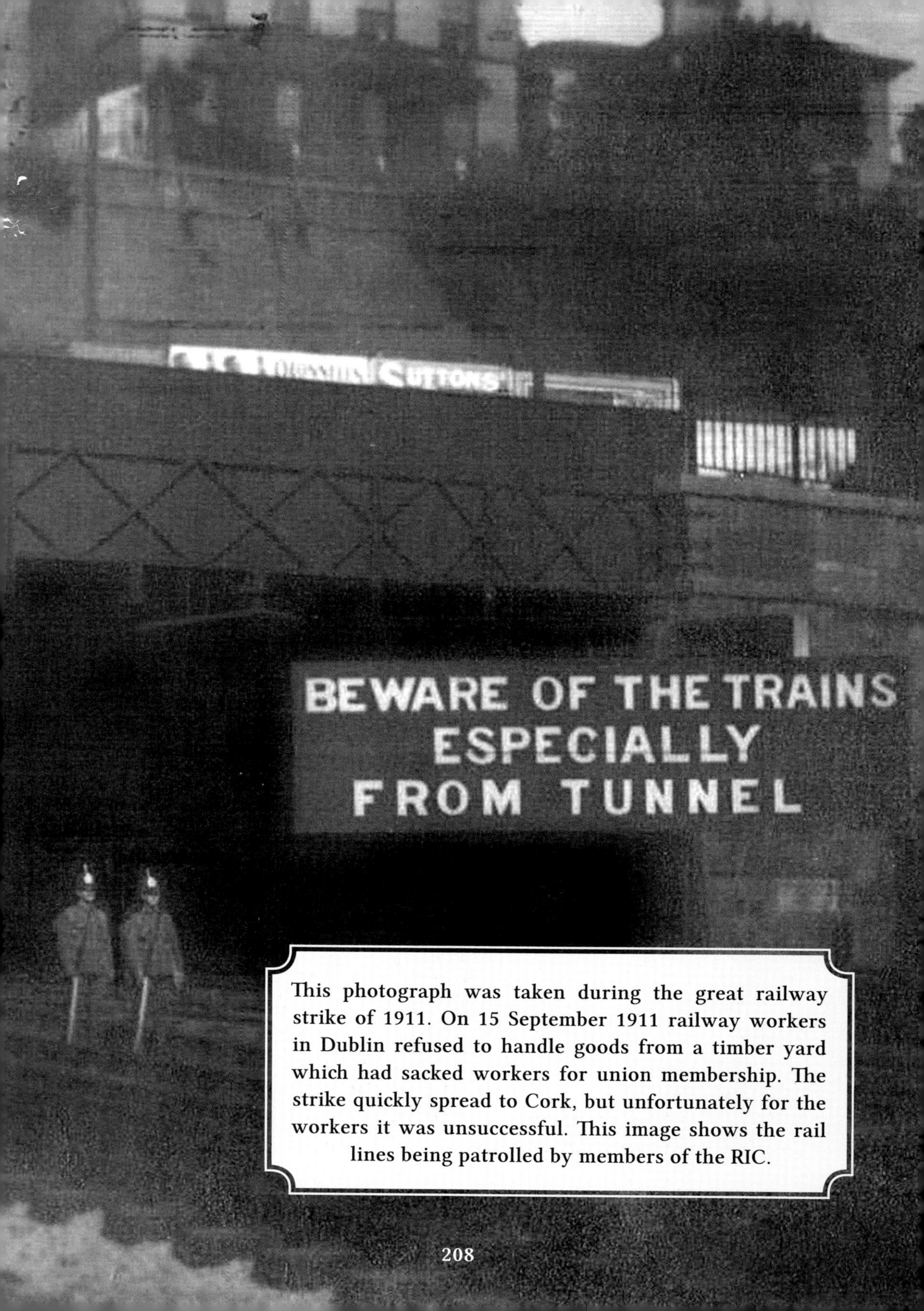

This photograph was taken during the great railway strike of 1911. On 15 September 1911 railway workers in Dublin refused to handle goods from a timber yard which had sacked workers for union membership. The strike quickly spread to Cork, but unfortunately for the workers it was unsuccessful. This image shows the rail lines being patrolled by members of the RIC.

A very rare view of the railway yard in the old Glanmire Station taken in 1896. Across the quays an old mill building appears quite ghostly.

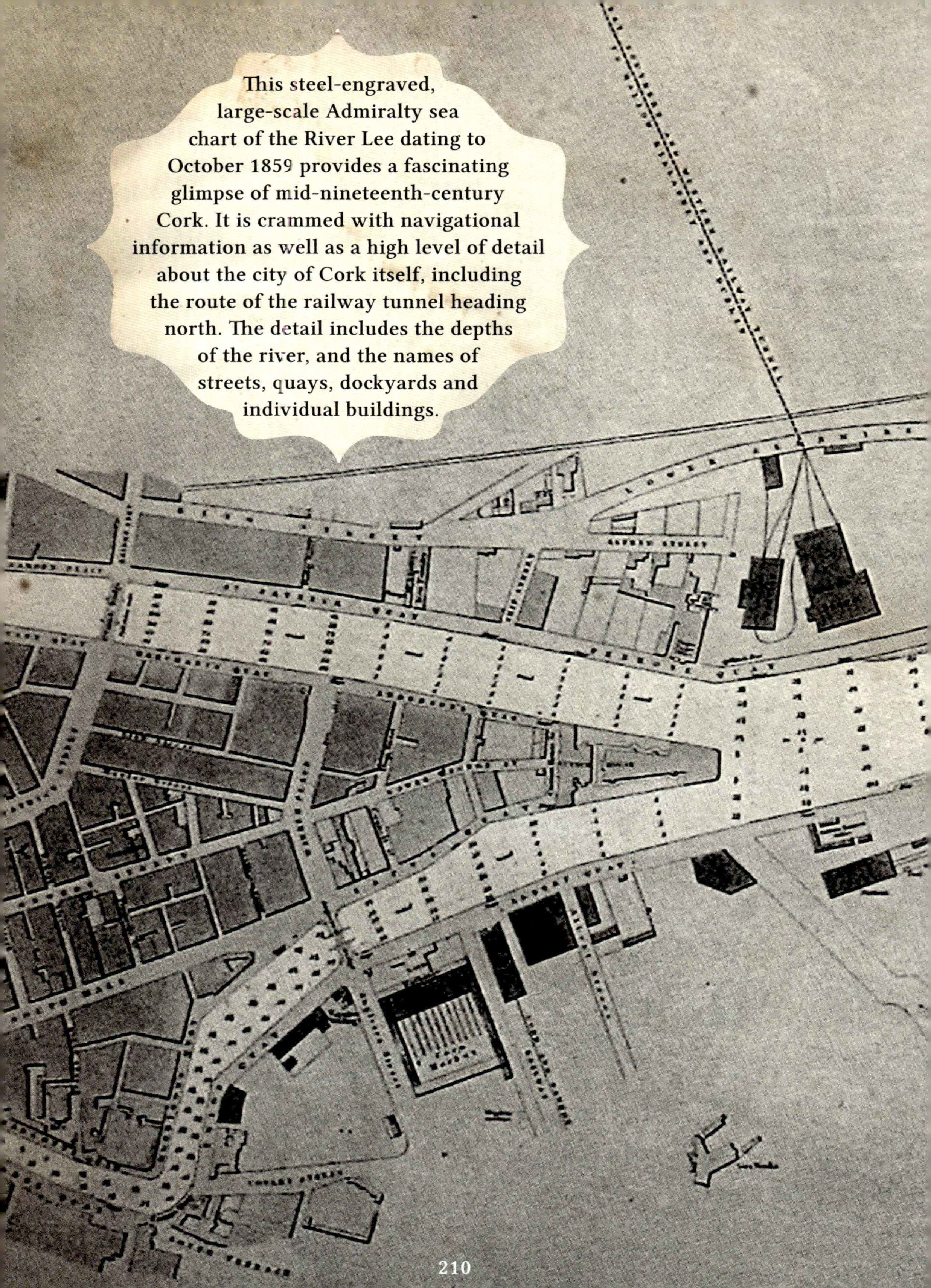

This steel-engraved, large-scale Admiralty sea chart of the River Lee dating to October 1859 provides a fascinating glimpse of mid-nineteenth-century Cork. It is crammed with navigational information as well as a high level of detail about the city of Cork itself, including the route of the railway tunnel heading north. The detail includes the depths of the river, and the names of streets, quays, dockyards and individual buildings.

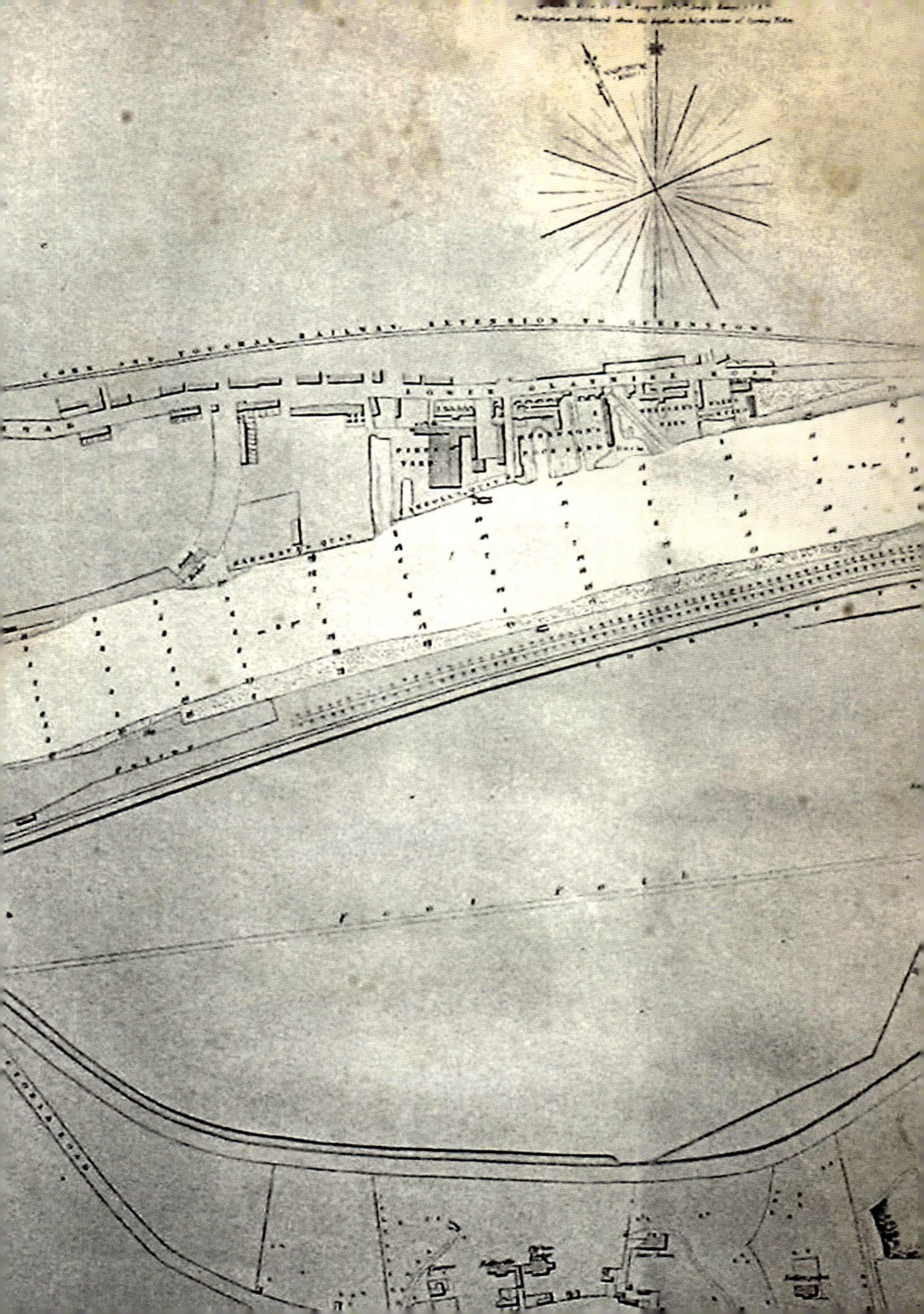
CORK AND YOUGHAL RAILWAY EXTENSION TO QUEENSTOWN
LOWER GLANMIRE ROAD
YARD

Our journey now takes us back into town along the quays. This postcard shows sailing ships on St Patrick's Quay. This was a very busy shipping quay where ships could discharge their cargoes in the heart of the city. This image also shows Brian Boru Railway Bridge which dates it to *c*. 1912.

This photograph of St Patrick's Quay shows where sailing ships and steamers loaded and discharged their cargoes at the limestone quay walls. This image was taken *c.* 1860 by Helmut Petschler, a German photographer who toured Britain and Ireland, and through his images left behind a wonderful record of the places he visited.

This American stereo view of 1903 shows an Edwardian boy looking over the River Lee towards the beautiful bow-fronted building on Camden Quay. St Mary's Priory (extreme left) and Shandon steeple complete the background.

The foundation stone of St Mary's Dominican Church on Pope's Quay was laid in 1832. The Protestant architect Kearns Deane designed the building and provided his service without charging any fee. The church is Neo-Classical, with Greek Ionic-style detailing. It opened for worship on 20 October 1839 and was blessed by Bishop John Murphy. Amongst those attending on the day was 'The Liberator' Daniel O'Connell.

A view of Lavitt's Quay from St Patrick's Quay. To the left is the lofty chimney shaft of Booth & Fox eiderdown manufacturers and hair and feather merchants (established in 1826). On 11 August 1949 this building caught fire, causing severe damage to almost three-quarters of the entire block of buildings. Just six years later the nearby Opera House was also destroyed by fire, changing the streetscape entirely.

In the 1940s Kyrl's Quay was a very industrious place, being home to sheet metal workers, furniture and cabinet makers, flour and meal dealers, and marine agents. One of Cork's oldest businesses, established in 1779, John Daly & Co. had its mineral water factory, stores and stables located here. This firm was responsible for creating the wonderful Cork tangerine drink Tanora in 1916.

MANUFACTURED ONLY BY
JOHN DALY & CO. Ltd.
Mineral Water Manufacturers, CORK.

"Tanora"

This hand-coloured view shows the premises of Bible Brothers on the far side of North Gate Bridge at the bottom of Shandon Street. This shop was known to generations of children and adults as Nosie O'Keeffe's, the finest sweet shop in Cork. Row upon row of glass jars containing every imaginable sweet and chocolate of every description was available to tantalise our young palates.

The old, beautiful and ornate cast-iron North Gate Bridge linking North Main Street and Shandon Street was opened in 1864. Unfortunately in 1964 it had to make way for a new concrete structure to accommodate the increased levels of traffic. The new bridge is called Griffith's Bridge, although it is still fondly known to many as North Gate Bridge.

The writer Frank O'Connor (real name Michael O'Donovan) was born on Douglas Street in Cork and spent his early childhood up to the age of five at No. 251 Blarney Street. This wonderful drawing of Blarney Street by William Harrington captures the community spirit, when many of the houses had half doors from which neighbours could communicate with each other. (*Courtesy of Denis Lenihan*)

(251) Blarney St. Cork
William Harrington ('85)

CORK 3974. W.L.

This view from the high ground above Blarney Street on the north side of Cork city gives us a wonderful panorama right down towards Lough Mahon. While you can see St Patrick's Bridge, the Brian Boru Railway Bridge had not been built when this photograph was taken, dating it to around the 1890s. The chimney shaft in the right foreground is the shaft of Wise's Distillery, which stood 160 feet high, dominating the skyline.

The famous steeple of Shandon, located in the heart of the Butter Exchange area. A committee of Cork merchants met at Rugg's Tavern on 5 May 1770 and a grading system for butter was adopted. This was the beginning of Cork's famous butter market. The quality of butter was graded on a scale of one to six – the worst quality (fifth and sixth) was referred to as grease. The Cork Butter Market existed from 1770 until 1924, when cheaper imports and the introduction of margarine forced its closure.

This is the old Butter Exchange building off Shandon Street, where the grading of Cork butter took place at 11 o'clock each morning and prices were agreed. Sir John Benson enlarged this building considerably between 1830 and 1850. The tradition of using this name is continued in the Butter Exchange Band, affectionately known as the Buttera. Formerly known as St Mary's Band, it was renamed in 1878.

An old Cork silver note, so-called because they replaced silver coins, issued by Daniel Foley, a grocer located at No. 2 Shandon Street. These small denomination notes were issued by local shopkeepers and could only be redeemed on their premises. Very few of these have survived to the present day.

This picture postcard view of Upper Cattle Market Street was taken in the 1950s. This picture was originally black and white, but was later coloured by the postcard studio.

Workers from the renowned bakery of Ormond & Ahern, 107 Shandon Street, are shown here proudly displaying their All Ireland Cup for the best bread in 1929, just three years after the bakery's foundation. Their exhibition bread was baked using water drawn from a spring at Nash's Boreen, ensuring that they had the edge over their competitors. (*Courtesy of Harry Ormond*)

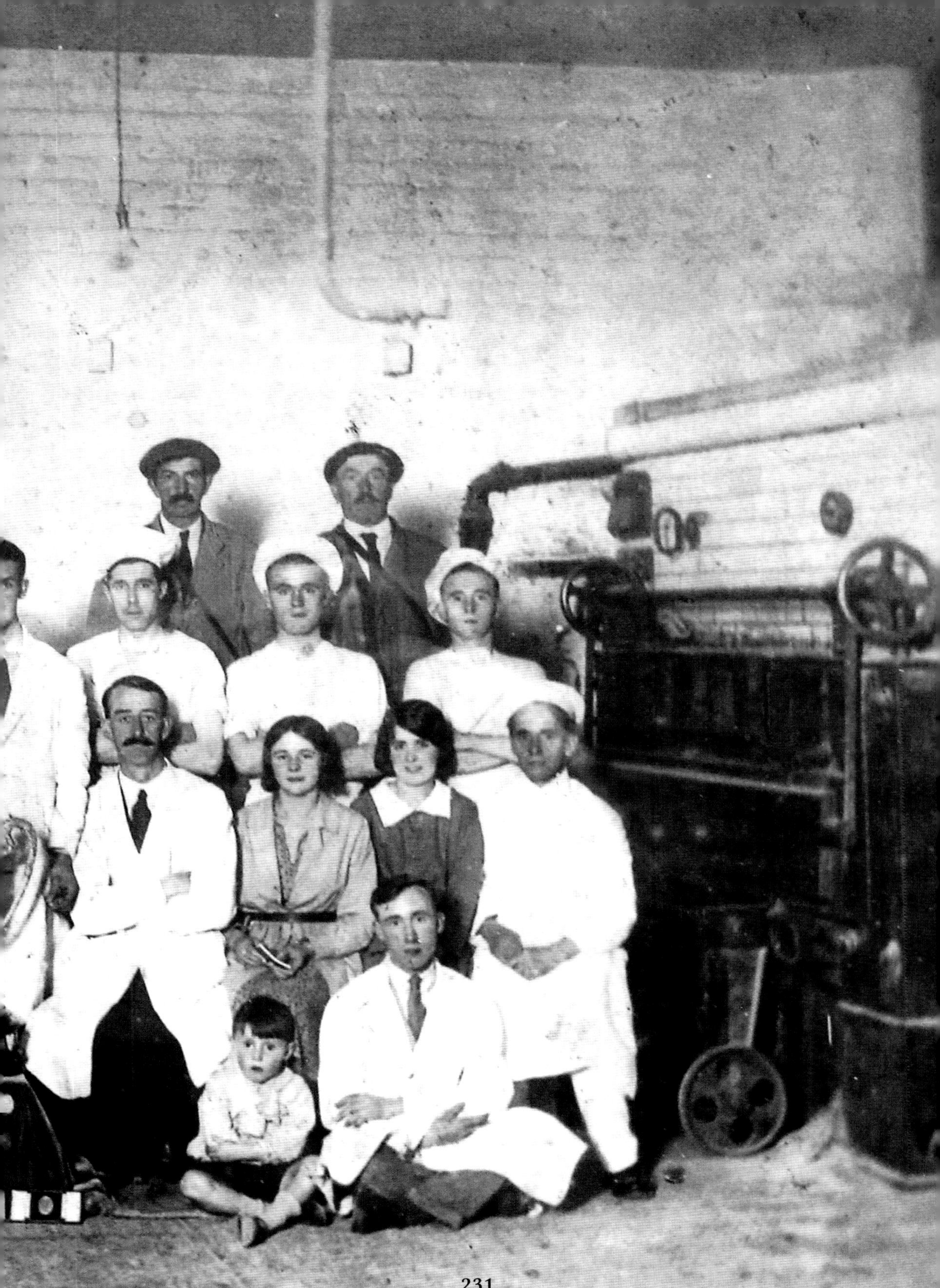

A wonderful view of the North Infirmary, John Redmond Street, in its heyday. The dental hospital, which was founded in 1913, was located across the road. Many a poor patient had their teeth removed at a time when excruciating pain was inflicted as the norm. (*Courtesy of the Daughters of Charity*)

This frontal view of the infirmary dates to 1914. Note the water feature and the portico at the front which no longer exist in the building's most recent incarnation as the Maldron Hotel. (*Courtesy of the Daughters of Charity*)

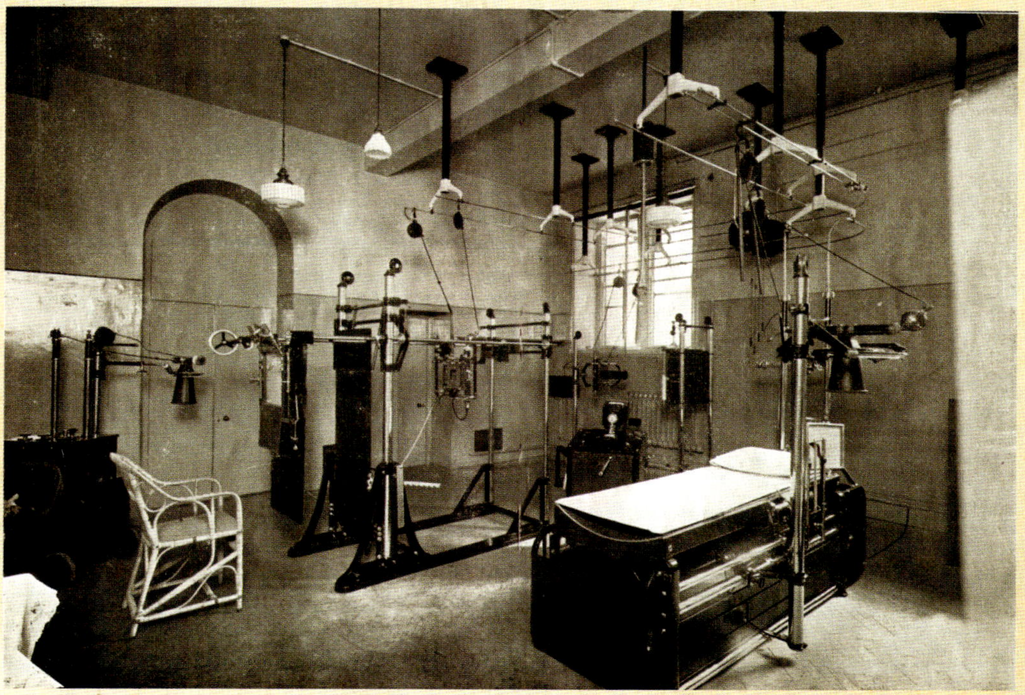

The X-ray department of the North Infirmary in 1938, a scene worthy of any Hammer horror film.

The Infirmary was founded in 1720 and in 1744 received the patronage of Dr Robert Clayton, Bishop of Cork. In 1752 an Act of Parliament officially established the North Infirmary, and a purpose-built facility was constructed on part of the grounds of the old Shandon graveyard.

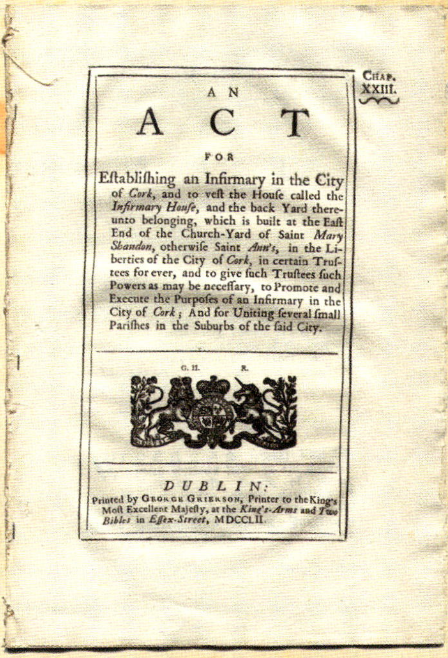

CHAP. XXIII.

AN

ACT

FOR

Eſtabliſhing an Infirmary in the City of *Cork*, and to veſt the Houſe called the *Infirmary Houſe*, and the back Yard thereunto belonging, which is built at the Eaſt End of the Church-Yard of Saint *Mary Shandon*, otherwiſe Saint *Ann's*, in the Liberties of the City of *Cork*, in certain Truſtees for ever, and to give ſuch Truſtees ſuch Powers as may be neceſſary, to Promote and Execute the Purpoſes of an Infirmary in the City of *Cork*; And for Uniting ſeveral ſmall Pariſhes in the Suburbs of the ſaid City.

G. II. R.

DUBLIN:

Printed by GEORGE GRIERSON, Printer to the King's Moſt Excellent Majeſty, at the *King's-Arms* and *Two Bibles* in *Eſſex-Street*, MDCCLII.

This stereo view of the North Cathedral dates to 1877. The North Cathedral was built in 1808, but was damaged by fire in 1828 and completely renovated by George Pain. The architect John Benson had ambitious plans for a 200-foot tower, which would have made it higher than St Anne's in Shandon, but this was never completed.

The 1905 infants' class of St Vincent's School, which was founded in 1857 off St Mary's Street. In May 1858 the building of a new primary school commenced and by December 1858 the children were transferred from a temporary building to the well-lit, ventilated, spacious schoolroom.

The old North Monastery building showing Our Lady's Mount in the background. The North Monastery was founded on 9 November 1811 by Brother Jerome O'Connor and Brother John Baptist Leonard. Built on a 14-acre site purchased from Sir John Gould in 1814, the building is no longer in existence.

A rare view of the chapel of the Sisters of Charity, which was located on Peacock Lane. The Magdalen Asylum was founded by Nicholas Therry for the reformation of 'penitent deluded females' on the 1 January 1800. The poor women were made to wash clothes, sew, spin and make quilts to earn their keep.

The old St Nicholas' Church, which was built in 1895 and was originally part of the Blackpool National School building. It was demolished in the 1940s to make way for the new Church of the Assumption. (*Courtesy of the Blackpool Historical Society*)

The Church of the Assumption, Blackpool, was designed by the notable Cork sculptor Seamus Murphy and celebrated its first Mass on 7 October 1945. William Dwyer, the owner of the Sunbeam textile factory, provided a large part of the funds for this building. For many years after it was opened it was known as 'Dwyer's fire escape'. Dwyer, although married, had a keen eye for the fairer sex and it was jokingly suggested that he built the church to keep his soul from the fires of hell.

A rare image of the Blackpool to Douglas tram, which ran from the city along the Watercourse Road and terminated at Blackpool Bridge near St Nicholas' Church. Near Murphy's Brewery there was a sharp corner where it is recorded that many an accident took place.

Crowds outside Tomás MacCurtain's shop at 40 Thomas Davis Street where he had a small clothing and rainwear business. On 20 March 1920, at just thirty-six years of age, he was murdered in front of his wife and family by members of the RIC. The coroner recorded the unusual verdict of wilful murder against the British Prime Minister David Lloyd George. (*Courtesy of Mercier Press*)

SUNBEAM LIMITED

The Sunbeam factory in Blackpool was a major employer on the north side of the city from 1928 until it closed in 1995. Originally the Millfield Mill, it was taken over by William Dwyer in 1928 for his textile business. A Sunbeam brochure boasted that the factory produced enough wool to stretch twice around the world. (*Courtesy of Blackpool Historical Society*)

FULLY FASHIONED KNITTING PLANT

In its heyday, Sunbeam employed over 3,000 people. The staff had access to free medical and dental care, as well as canteen facilities which provided hot meals, chocolate and cigarettes. Sport also played a big part in the social calendar, and recreation grounds were provided where many football matches took place. A huge fire destroyed the main building in 2003. (*Courtesy of Blackpool Historical Society*)

The beautiful ornate entrance gates to Murphy's Brewery on the Watercourse Road. A fully laden horse and dray makes its way carefully onto the road guided by its drayman. The firm had its own horses, and its stables were located on the opposite side of the road.

LADYS WELL
LADY'S WELL BREWERY

The triumvirate of the Shandon steeple, Murphy's Brewery chimney and the North Cathedral dominate the skyline in this picture postcard. Even though Murphy's Brewery was established in 1856, the chimney was not constructed until the 1870s. Unfortunately, due to health and safety fears, the chimney was demolished in 1985 and a little piece of Cork history vanished from the skyline. *Inset:* A prize medal from the old foundling hospital which existed on the site prior to the brewery.

Foundling
HOSPITAL
Cork

An extremely rare postcard of Coburg Street, which was once known as Maddens Field. This area was used by cattle dealers to hold livestock prior to its departure to England. The name Coburg derives from the Saxe-Coburg dynasty, to which the British royal family were related.

57 C. CARROLL 57

St Patrick's Hill *c.* 1912, one of the steepest gradients in Cork. In former days messenger boys on their bicycles used to race each other down this hill right into the city – certainly not something for the faint-hearted. Today it is often used during cycle racing events, providing a mammoth endurance test for the competitors.

The Cork Grammar School was founded in 1882 and later became the merged Cork High School & Kindergarten. It was originally located at Sydney Place, shown here. On 3 September 1917 the Cork Grammar School was raided by the IRB and a substantial amount of ammunition, Lee-Enfield rifles and thirty swords were stolen. These weapons had been used in training by the Voluntary Training Corps. The school relocated to Blackrock in 1956 and became part of Ashton School in 1972.

This photograph shows the Royal Welsh Guards on parade at Victoria Barracks (now Collins Barracks), complete with their goat mascot. This photograph was taken on 18 July 1909 at the staff parade whilst the front rank are inspected.

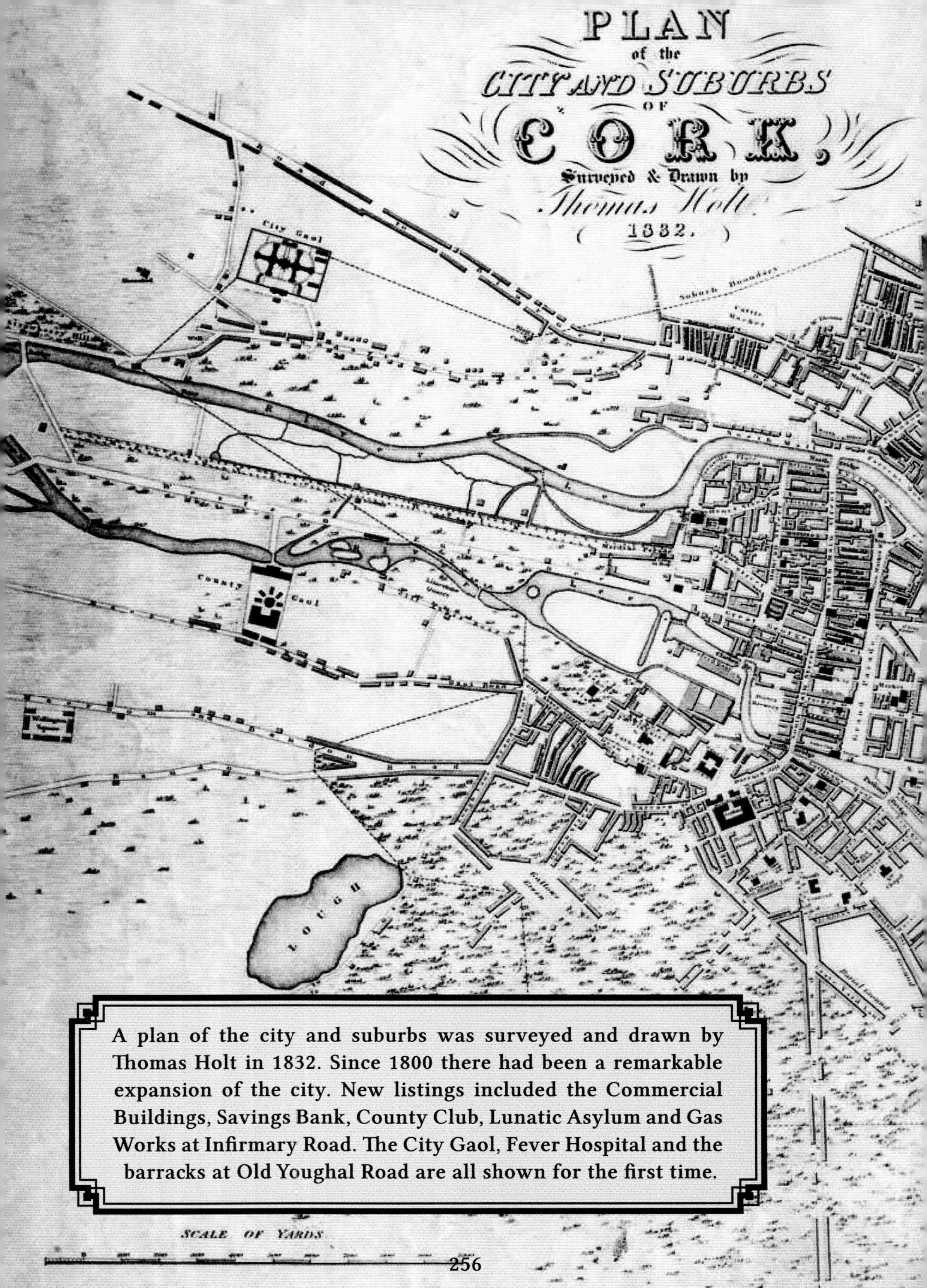

A plan of the city and suburbs was surveyed and drawn by Thomas Holt in 1832. Since 1800 there had been a remarkable expansion of the city. New listings included the Commercial Buildings, Savings Bank, County Club, Lunatic Asylum and Gas Works at Infirmary Road. The City Gaol, Fever Hospital and the barracks at Old Youghal Road are all shown for the first time.

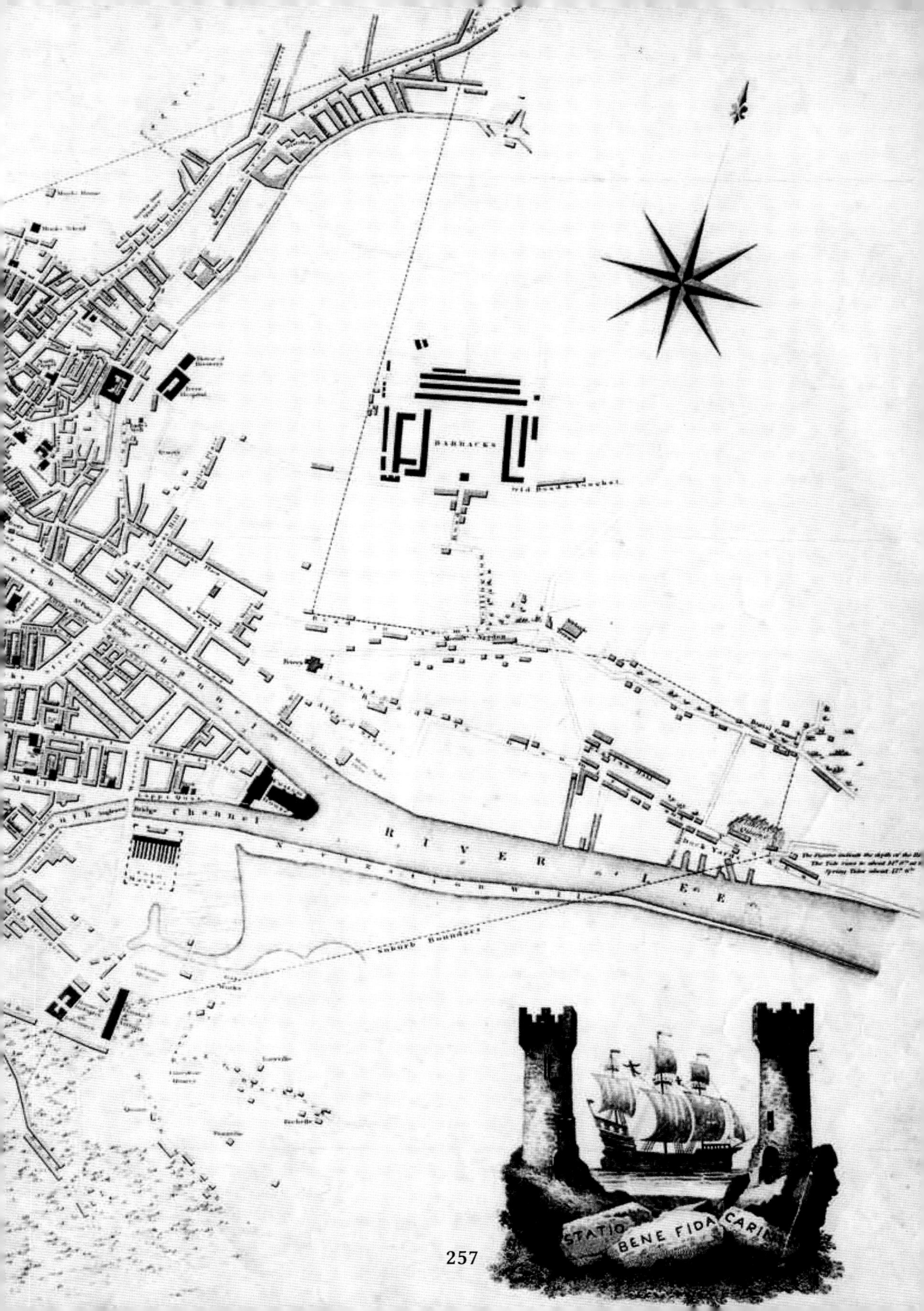
BARRACKS
RIVER
LEE
STATIO
BENE FIDA

Cousin Harry

Below: An extremely early photograph of the old guardroom at Victoria Barracks, taken by Captain Henry Craigie Brewster *c.* 1843. This is probably the oldest Cork photograph in existence. The old guardroom was designed by John Gibson in 1806.

Left: An image of the officers' mess in Victoria Barracks, 1906.

A picture of a First World War volunteer nurse who was working at Victoria Barracks during the 1914–1918 period. She is identified on the reverse as Miss A. R. Price, VAD. The Voluntary Aid Detachment (VAD) provided field nursing, driving and cooking services during the war, mainly in hospitals in the United Kingdom and various other countries in the British Empire.

The garrison church of Victoria Barracks which was built in 1850. It had a section which was used as a school for the children of military personnel of all denominations. This church later became known as St Michael's.

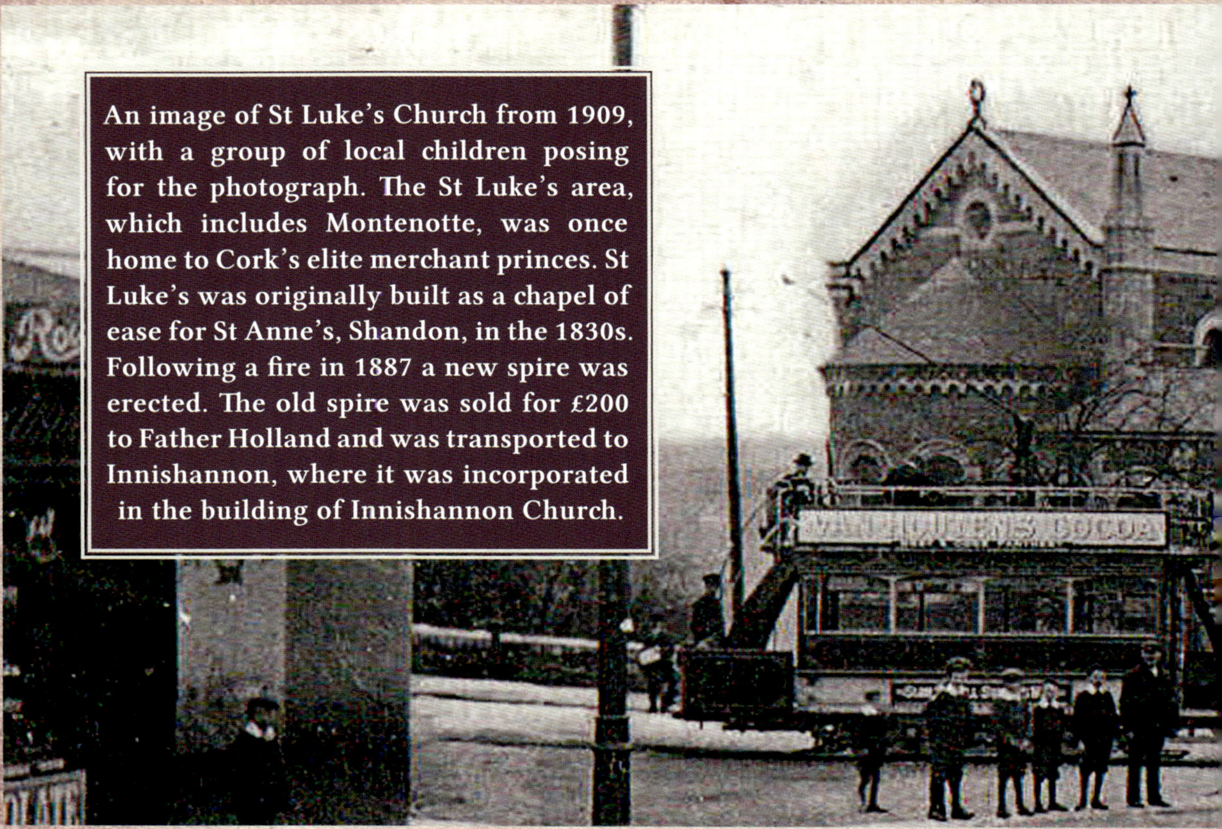

An image of St Luke's Church from 1909, with a group of local children posing for the photograph. The St Luke's area, which includes Montenotte, was once home to Cork's elite merchant princes. St Luke's was originally built as a chapel of ease for St Anne's, Shandon, in the 1830s. Following a fire in 1887 a new spire was erected. The old spire was sold for £200 to Father Holland and was transported to Innishannon, where it was incorporated in the building of Innishannon Church.

The Little Sisters of the Poor in Montenotte was a charitable institution that was home to women and men over sixty years. In 2002 the building was sold and has now been renovated to a high standard as Care Choice Montenotte nursing home.

A view of Tivoli showing a sailing boat on the tranquil waters of the River Lee. From the mid 1800s, this stretch of the river was used to stage the Cork City Regatta. Various boat clubs were formed about this time, including the Lee Rowing Club in 1858, Cork Harbour Rowing Club in 1859, Queen's College Cork Rowing Club in 1866 and Cork Boat Club in 1899.

The large houses of some of the merchants of the city in Montenotte and Tivoli peer down on this tranquil scene. To the left is the twenty-five-to-one gun, a cannon from the Crimean War captured during the siege of Sebastopol. This cannon was fired at 12.35 p.m. local time every day, the equivalent of 1 p.m. Greenwich Mean Time, signalling the time difference between Britain and Ireland.

From Tivoli we head back into town along Penrose Quay. This postcard shows a busy scene outside the St George Steam Packet Co. on the quay. Many of this company's ships were destroyed by German submarines during the First World War. The first *Innisfallen* was one such victim. *Inset:* Cover of a brochure from 1924 for the City of Cork Steam Packet Co.

The wide expanse of Penrose and St Patrick's Quays, and to the left the steamships of the Cork Steam Ship Co., which was responsible for commissioning the first crossing of the Atlantic by a paddle steamer, the *Sirius*. Many of the company's ships were named after birds, such as the *Bittern*, *Fulmar*, *Egret*, *Dodo* and the *Kittiwake*. These ships would have been a common sight on the river at the turn of the twentieth century.

The SS *Classic* arrived in Cork in May 1921 and serviced the Fishguard crossing for the Cork Steam Packet Co., based on Penrose Quay. In August 1922 she was requisitioned to take the body of General Michael Collins to Dublin after he had been killed at Béal Na Bláth, because rail transport had been curtailed during the Civil War. In 1924 her name was changed to the *Killarney*. She continued in service until 1948 when she was scrapped.

A 1938 advertising card showing the second *Innisfallen*, which also plied the Cork to Fishguard route and docked on Penrose Quay. This ship had a respectable speed of 18 knots and had the latest features available for the comfort of its passengers. Unfortunately the ship was sunk during the Second World War.

An advertising postcard for the Cork Steam Packet Co. ship *Killarney*, just one of the many steamers to bear that name. The first ship to bear the name Killarney was a paddle steamer which sank near Rennie Bay, close to Roberts Cove, in 1838.

Brian Boru Bridge just before its completion. Brian Boru and Clontarf bridges were Scherzler rolling lift bascule bridges, constructed in 1911 to carry the railway over the river, whilst still allowing shipping access upriver when they were in the elevated position. This photograph was taken just weeks prior to the opening of the bridge. The final locomotives crossed this bridge at the end of September 1976, when Albert Quay, the only station still functioning on the south side of the river, was closed to rail traffic.

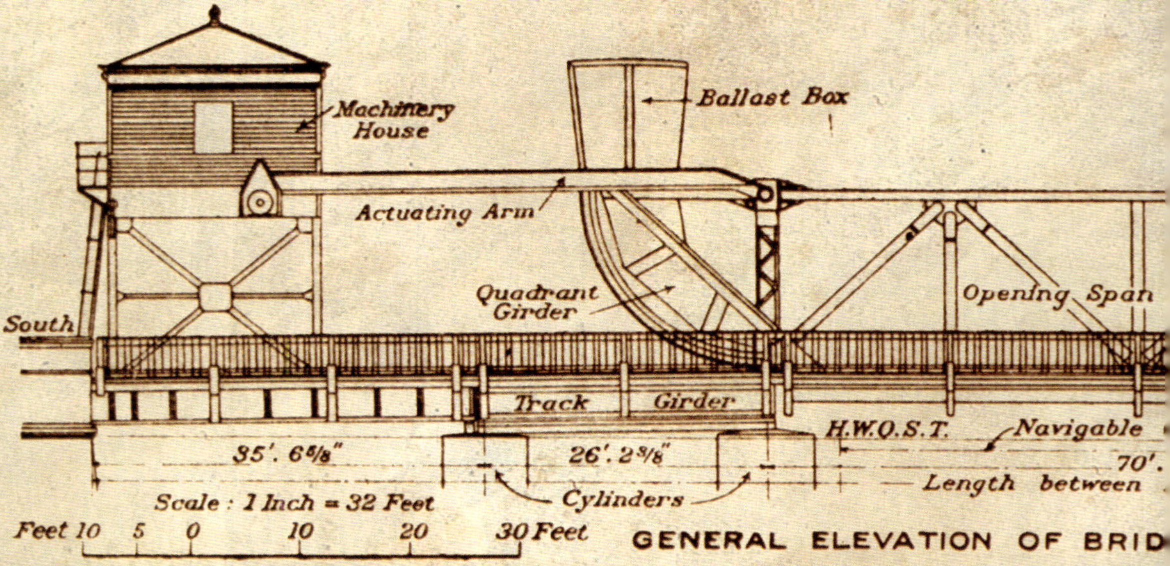

This sketch dates to 1932 when repairs were carried out on both the railway lifting bridges over the River Lee. After twenty years in operation and approximately 18,000 operations, serious maintenance was carried out by the Cork engineering firm Merrick's.

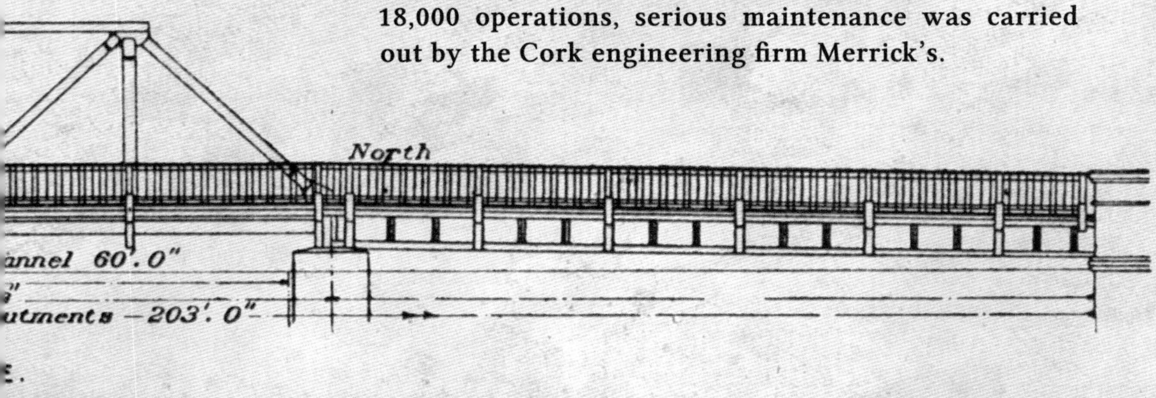

Here we see Locomotive 217 crossing Brian Boru Bridge in the 1950s. It is hard to imagine today that locomotives and wagons crossed the river and travelled through the heart of the city as part of the traffic. Woe betide any cyclist or motorcyclist who caught his front wheel in the tracks, as a nasty fall was sure to ensue! (*Courtesy of the Walter McGrath collection*)

On 2 December 1817 a public meeting was held at the Cork Commercial Rooms to establish a Trustee Savings Bank. The bank opened for business at the Cork Institution a fortnight later. Its first official headquarters was opened on Pembroke Street in 1824, but it moved to a custom-built premises on Lapp's Quay in 1842. The Lapp's Quay building was designed by the Deane brothers and completed on 20 August 1842 for the then considerable sum of £11,000.

An old steam locomotive trundling across Clontarf Bridge. Note the railway worker carrying a flag and walking in front of the locomotive. The Railway Act of 1856 required that a man, complete with red flag or lantern, had to walk sixty yards ahead to warn horse-drawn traffic of the approach of a self-propelled machine. At that time the speed limit was set at between two and four miles per hour. The practice of the flag carrying continued up to the close of the bridges to railway traffic.

A railway map from the 1920s of the different railway routes and stations, with the inset showing the city routes in more detail and the two railway bridges across the Lee. Cork was very fortunate in having many private railway companies. The Cork & Muskerry Light Railway, the Macroom Direct Railway, the Cork, Bandon & South Coast Railway, and the Cork, Blackrock & Passage Railway all operated within the city.

A view of Lapp's Quay and the Clontarf Bridge in December 1911 prior to its official opening just two weeks later. The design drawings of the bridge were drafted by the famous Glasgow civil engineering business, Sir William Arrol & Co. Ltd. Originally both the Clontarf and Brian Boru bridges were painted red, but they are now a battleship grey colour.

A wonderful aerial view of the city which can be dated to the early 1930s as the building of the new City Hall is not yet complete. This was an important time in Cork's history, as many significant city centre premises were being rebuilt following the desolation of December 1920, including Roche's Stores, Cash's, the Munster Arcade and Egan's.

An early stereo view *c.* 1870 of a sailing ship moored outside the old city hall, which had started life as the Cornmarket or Corn Exchange in 1833. The first Cork Exhibition took place there in 1852. Following the second Cork Exhibition of 1883 it became the Municipal Buildings. In 1906 a town hall was constructed to house the great organ from the 1902/03 exhibitions and it then became the official City Hall.

An original photograph of the new City Hall designed by Jones and Kelly, taken shortly after it was completed by the local building firm of Sisk & Co. The foundation stone was laid by Taoiseach Éamon de Valera in 1932 and it was officially opened by him in 1936.

The beautiful three-masted barque the *Killoran* was a regular visitor to Cork in the 1930s, when this photograph was taken on Kennedy Quay. Unfortunately she was sunk by the German cruiser *Widder* in August 1940. The German surgeon on board pressurised the captain to sink her so that he could film the sinking. The *Killoran*'s crew watched helplessly as explosives blew her apart. (*Courtesy of Charlie Ginnane*)

Our last image is also of Kennedy Quay. This photograph was taken during the 1930s. Horse-drawn transport is still very much evident in this scene, although the Leyland lorry heralds the new era of motor transport that would soon see scenes like this disappear. The massive sailing ship in the background serves as a reminder of the glory days of sail, when these majestic ships transported cargoes from Cork all over the world. (*Courtesy of Charlie Ginnane*)

Index